LIGHT IN THE JUNGLE

LIGHT IN THE JUNGLE

*The Thirty Years' Mission of Leo and
Jessie Halliwell along the Amazon*

by LEO B. HALLIWELL

Edited and with a Foreword by
WILL OURSLER

DAVID McKAY COMPANY, Inc.
New York

Library of Congress Catalogue Card Number: 59-9386

MANUFACTURED IN THE UNITED STATES OF AMERICA

CONTENTS

ILLUSTRATIONS

following page 50

FOREWORD

IT was something like a scene in a dream—the lush green of the jungle, the vivid golden yellow of the waters lapping against the banks, the deep blue of the sky beyond, a blue that was different from our Vermont sky—deeper, more translucent, more mysterious. And yet it was here—the Amazon itself, in all its color and glory, against the wall of a century-old farmhouse overlooking the quiet hills and woods in the town of Adamant, Vermont, where I have my summer home.

On the wall of this farmhouse was another world, another continent, half a hemisphere away. As I watched, I glided with the camera down a dark stream past a jungle that seemed to reach out with its shadows, its deceptive fingers clutching—even at this great distance, in this motion picture thrown against the wall.

The scenes were unlike any I had ever watched before, in travelogues, magazines, or guidebooks. These were not pictures taken by tourists. Here was a line of the sick waiting to board a boat, one by one, to be treated. This one had the yaws and the woman is giving him an injection. The woman is Mrs. Halliwell—Dona Jessie, as she was known along the river.

Here is another youngster, sun-tanned and bright-eyed.

Yet his leg is terribly swollen and deformed, and his little body grotesquely misshapen.

Out of the darkness of the Vermont room where we watched this picture, I hear the voice of Leo Halliwell—Senhor Leo, the river folk called him. "That youngster was too sick, too far gone, for us to save him," he said. "We did all we could, but we reached him too late."

Here is a scene of a minor operation on the little medical boat that these two people—the Halliwells—used on the Amazon. For more than a quarter of a century this white launch was their home, and consulting room, and clinic, as they traveled through streams and tropic torrents to serve these people, to bring them health and guidance.

"Back in the Middle West where I grew up," Leo Halliwell was saying, "when I was just a young man about to start out on all this, one of my friends warned me that I was throwing away my life."

His laughter filled the room. "That man was a good friend and he is now a big industrialist. He was trying to keep me from this work in Brazil because he didn't think it would pay off for me or Jessie, but it has—a thousand times over."

Not in money, I knew that. The Halliwells are certainly not wealthy people. They are average, everyday Americans like those on any main street in any town in America. Graying now, growing a little older, overweight a little, more conscious of their years. Their children are grown with families of their own—their daughter with her doctor husband in Texas, their son working in the American Embassy in Rio.

And so they had come to my home in Vermont. They were telling me about their work. But the pictures, brilliant against the white wall, were more than a traveler's collection of movie films. They were a record of two people who had given a lifetime of service as medical missionaries in the *Inferno Verde*—the Green Hell of the Amazon. This man and woman out of Nebraska, out of the cornfields and the wheatfields and the endless prairies, had gone into the jungle to serve their fellow man, to help make him well, to bring him the word of faith and the love of God.

They had gone where not too many others dared go. Fevers and insects, snakes, wild animals, plagues and epidemics, storms and savage Indians—none of these had kept them from this work through more than twenty-seven years along these rivers. There, in my Vermont living room, Leo rolled out a snakeskin for me to see. It was almost thirty feet long and three and one half feet wide. "We found the snake under our building," Leo said, "and we had to shoot it dead."

The river changed in the years that they were there. The people who had been in the grip of every imaginable tropical disease are healthier and happier, and living with new hope and new ambitions and new futures. For much of this change the Halliwells are responsible. So much so that the government of Brazil awarded them the Brazilian Cross for their work.

These were the people who had come to me with their story. It is still their story. They lived it; they told it.

I have heard many adventures in my life and have written many and have lived through a few adventures, too; but none compare to the tale which this couple spun for me. The scope of their work was a continent; their people were like a nation apart, forgotten, swallowed up in the jungle shadows.

This was the setting of the story as for a generation they roamed the waterways of the Amazon and mingled with its people, bringing medicine and healing where they were needed, counsel and advice, wisdom and patience and charity, as a counteraction to violence and poisoned arrows and disease and murder.

To one of the most beautiful, fantastic, unbelievably exciting and violent places on the face of the earth, in unknown, unexplored byways, they brought their message of faith, their word of hope, and their store of freely given medicine to help these people in body and mind and in the dignity of the spirit.

Their story is one that is unique because so few people would have dared to live it. But it is a story that I knew had to be told and told, insofar as possible, in their own terms, in their own way. At times this saga may seem rough and even brutal. At times it may seem unbelievable. But all of these things happened to them in the life that they found in the Amazon world.

While we were working together, they took a little house nearby for a few weeks and Dona Jessie set up house-keeping. One night she said, "Come over to the boat to-night for dinner."

Of course, there was no boat, this was only a farmhouse close by our own in the hills. But somehow, somewhere, in this Vermont hill country Dona Jessie had found the ingredients for a Brazilian dinner.

It was an exciting, even an exotic evening, that blend of Brazil and the backwoods of New England. We had never tasted a meal more delicious, and somehow as we ate and talked and Dona Jessie moved so easily around the room to give us extra helpings of everything, it was not too hard to imagine that we really were on the boat, that it really was Brazil, and that just outside the windows was the Amazon with its alligators, its man-eating piranhas, its giant bullfrogs in the shadows of the soaring trees along the riverbanks.

WILL OURSLER

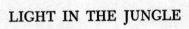

LIGHT IN THE JUNGLE

CHAPTER 1

A RIVER AT NIGHT

NIGHT had come on the Amazon. It had come, as always to this river, suddenly, swiftly, precisely at six o'clock, with no twilight at all. Throughout the whole day we had treated the sick in an improvised clinic on the porch of a house by the riverbank. The malaria fever had been bad all along the Amazon that year, particularly in this area to which we had come in our boat, the *Luzeiro*— the name is a Portuguese Biblical word meaning Bearer of Light. The people had been waiting for us, waving their white towels as they saw us coming upriver. On the banks they had collected their sick, people of all ages, many of them dying or almost dead.

So we had set up our clinic, my wife, Jessie, and I. Word of our arrival with our medicines had spread quickly; canoes had seemed to come from all directions, swarming to this place, filled with men and women and children in pitiful condition, some with their bodies grotesquely enlarged or deformed from the terrible disease known in Brazil as malignant malaria.

One fisherman that day brought to us in his canoe a little child who was suffering from this fever. He had found the child in a hut at the edge of a village a few miles up the river. The child had been alone in the insect-

3

infested abode. No one knew what had happened to his parents or any others of his family. We gave treatment, and the kindly fisherman promised to take care of this child who was too weak even to tell us his name.

It was late in the afternoon when we treated the last of these patients, and Jessie was weary after the long grueling day. We pulled up anchor and moved a short distance downstream into a kind of lake connected to the main part of the river by a narrow stream only a few yards long but deep enough for our launch. We came into a beautiful place where the water was still and dark and deep, with the main currents of the Amazon sweeping past only a short distance away. Here, for the night, we retreated into our own moment of quiet.

The pattern of the evening began. The boat boy bestirred himself with chores out on deck and the boat girl began to prepare our evening meal. Jessie rested in her bunk. Through the cabin window I watched the sunset: the color had deepened to crimson, the reflection in the still lake was like a mirror of vermilion, broken only where tall palms that lined the bank threw long shadows far out on the water. Flamingoes and parrots winged by, on their way to their nests for the night. Now the crimson hue faded, the sun was gone, darkness closed in. Later, I remember, the moon rose, almost at the full that night, big and bright, throwing a soft silver haze across the lake and the Amazon River beyond.

I lay awake in the dark of the cabin. Jessie and the others by then were asleep in their bunks. The hush of darkness was broken by a thousand familiar sounds of the Amazon night, the strange symphony which had become so familiar to us that usually we did not hear it at all. There were the mingling sounds of the giant bullfrog and leaping fish, the cry of a monkey or a bird, the sudden throaty grunt of the alligator, the snorting of the dulpan, which always reminded me of the horses on our farm back in Nebraska. The melody of the darkness on the river was a constant thing.

Day or night, this world of the Amazon and the dense, trackless, largely untrodden jungles that reach out over half a continent is a world of sounds. An insect stops his song, a bird stirs, a tropical leaf rustles. Loud and soft, these half-heard sounds may mean life or death. Living on this great river, you learn to live by these sounds instinctively, without hearing them.

In the cool darkness of our boat, against the symphony of night outside, my thoughts drifted across this river world that had been our home and was to remain so for many years. Half a lifetime has passed since we came to this world of Brazil out of the corn belt of Nebraska, where both Jessie and I had grown up. We were to come to know these people, to work with them and try to aid them where they needed help, to love them and to be a part of their lives, so that we, as medical missionaries on the Amazon River, were almost as much Brazilian as the Brazilians themselves.

As I lay quietly, listening to the sounds of the night, my thoughts went back many years to a Sabbath morning in Rio de Janeiro. For the first time we had gone to a service of our church there that day—the Seventh-day Adventist Church, of which we were missionaries. It was a lovely, sunlit church, beautiful in its simplicity. As we sat in worship, into the pew beside us came a man and woman, carrying with them, on a brightly embroidered satin pillow, a baby. It was so tiny that Jessie turned to me and whispered, "Look, Leo—that infant couldn't be more than a week or so old and they're bringing her to church already."

All through the service the baby lay sleeping on the pillow. Little Olga, they told us, after the service, was only two weeks old. Her father had come from Germany and her mother from Italy to work in our church, first in the Brazilian state of Baía and later in the city of Belém, where we made our headquarters, near the mouth of the Amazon. But we had no idea, as Jessie took the tiny baby into her arms, that years later this infant would be sharing intimately our work and our lives.

As I reflected on our work on the river, it was hard to distinguish one year and one season from another. It was as if we lived in a dream where the past and future merged and crisscrossed like the river shadows themselves. It was almost as difficult to distinguish between our many roles. We were minister and doctor, psychiatrist and matchmaker, salvager of marriages, godparents to a thousand children, a large percentage of whom Jessie herself had helped to bring into the world.

We had been godparents to the "nationals," as all descendants of the original Portuguese were called, no matter how mixed their blood had become. We were godparents to the children of the native Indians. For the people of the river, nationals or Indians, half-breeds or untamed, murder-spawned savages, had become our people. We had made ourselves a part of them and of this jungle world. We shared with them its joy and its beauty and its misery and pain, and we sought to bring help and healing and a new vision of our life and its meaning in terms of the love of God.

Many years have passed since that night I lay thinking and remembering in the cabin of the *Luzeiro*. The malaria, that dread disease of the tropics, has all but been wiped out. Perhaps, I sometimes say to myself, Jessie and I have helped. It is sure that, along the river, we are given such credit.

Only recently, a tall Brazilian national, his four sons towering about him, boarded our boat as we anchored at a small, isolated river community. It was obvious that he was an important citizen. He turned to Jessie, who stood beside me on the deck, and asked politely, "Dona Jessie, do you remember these boys?"

Dona Jessie looked at Senhor Leo—these are the names by which we are known along the river—and both of us shook our heads. At a thousand different points along the great stream we had treated tens of thousands of people. Try as we might, we could not remember them all. The father knew this, of course. But he persisted. "You ought to remember them, Dona Jessie. Were it not for you, they would all be dead."

He paused, then went on with a smile, "Years ago you and this boat stopped before my house. They were sick, all of my boys. They were nearly dead with malaria, and the youngest here was still only a baby. You stayed all that day and treated them and saved their lives."

I write of this now when malaria is no longer a major problem along the river. But that night, when I lay in the dark of the cabin, malaria was still one of the great killers throughout the Amazon and much of northern Brazil.

Jessie and I have seen many changes come. In some

measure we have helped to effect these changes. Although we were officially missionaries, we saw at once the diseases rampant on the Amazon and we knew that we had first to concentrate on making these people well before we could hope to convert them to any meaningful religion. We had not come to impose by force or fear our ideas or culture or dogmas; we had come to help other human beings. This was our assignment. To do this we had to become a part of the ways and the lives of these people. We learned their language and customs and traditions; we became truly Brazilian. We thought, spoke, even dreamed in Portuguese, the official language of the land.

We served these people throughout that land, from the cities of the south to the wildest areas of the great river, as we were guided to serve. In the most primitive districts, in the dark regions of the River of Roosevelt—once known as the River of Doubt—and the deadly fringes of the River of Death, we came not as enemies or would-be exploiters or hunters or adventurers; we came to help with our medicines and our schools and our teachers. And these people, some of them known as killer Indians, who had never before allowed white men upon their lands, accepted us. Today, in the very heart of this so-called perilous jungle, are our schools and our church and our teaching.

Throughout this river world a new day had begun.

Children who once would have grown up naked savages, whose little bodies were wracked with yaws and hookworm and other terrible diseases, are today well and healthy. They are clothed. They are attending schools, and preparing for high school and even college. Diseases that were rampant in the Amazon Valley have been wiped out or brought under control. In many places across this vast wilderness there are schools and churches, hospitals and clinics, new ideas and new understanding of sanitation and hygiene, new health among the people, new hope and new meaning. A world awakens, the great, sprawling, wonderful world of the continental valley called the Amazon.

Moments and incidents crowded my thoughts that night, as they have many nights since. A time when the frogs leaped from every direction during my meeting and my congregation fled in terror. A child lying naked on the floor, in a house full of the dead. An aged, withered chief who had stonily rejected all the help we tried to give him and his people, but who came to us at last and fell on his knees, tears of joy streaming down the thousand wrinkles of his face. A child groveling in a hogpen because a witch doctor insisted this was the way to drive out the devil that was making her ill. A three-year-old youngster mangled to death by an alligator before the parents could reach the child.

This was our work and our life for thirty-seven years. The perils we faced, the achievements and failures and challenges and difficulties—none of them could we have guessed in advance. But throughout all that time, wherever we were—on the *Luzeiro* or on some mission in the jungle itself—from the very beginning, we placed our trust unwaveringly in the protection of God. Never once in all that time, in the moments of greatest danger or difficulty, did we doubt that protection; never once did it fail.

Strange things have happened to us. Long ago we grew used to coincidences that are perhaps not coincidences at all.

In the city of Manaus, a thousand miles from the mouth

of the Amazon, a great modern city entirely surrounded by the Green Hell of the jungle, is a magnificent hotel, the Amazonas, equipped with every luxury anyone could imagine. The owner of this luxurious establishment came to us, one day when we were in Manaus, and introduced himself. "I have been trying to get in touch with you for weeks," he explained. "It is about an experience I had a few weeks ago in the lobby of the Waldorf-Astoria Hotel in New York City."

A young woman had come up to him, he said, holding in her hand a small box, and asking for a contribution for a special charity campaign of our church.

"I gave her fifty cents," he said. "Then, as she turned away, it suddenly came to me, very positively, that I ought to give this woman more than those few pennies. I called her back, drew out of my pocket a fifty-dollar bill, and handed it to her.

"She seemed quite overwhelmed. She gave me a copy of a magazine—one of your church's publications. On the cover was a photograph. It was a picture of your boat—tied up at my plantation here on the river, giving medical treatment to my workers.

"While the woman was thanking me for my gift, she was giving me something that meant much more—a lesson in the meaning of love and care. I didn't know about your boat or your work with these people. So I had to find you, you see—to thank you."

We were a long way from Manaus or New York, with their luxurious hotels, when we encountered another of these coincidences—one which made us more certain than ever of God's all-seeing eye.

It was our first trip up the river in our own boat, heading

west from Belém. I was new to navigation, unused to the river, and unaware of the location of shoals and dangerous rocks that could destroy us. A river pilot could have guided us safely through, but a pilot is a professional man and earns a good deal more than we or any missionary could afford to pay. As neophytes on the river, we had no choice but to feel our way along and trust we would be guided.

In some areas the river is fairly well populated along the banks. This is particularly so in the tidal areas within a few hundred miles of the mouth. There canoes come and go frequently, and at times we could see dozens of them going upstream close to the banks or downstream farther out in the river. Often the occupants would ask us to tow them along behind our boat; but because there were frequently so many and we couldn't take them all, we established from the start a policy of no hitchhiking.

Yet on this very first trip we broke our rule. We had reached a desolate area where the jungle closed in deep and green along the banks and there was no sign at all of habitation, only a kind of forlorn tropic hush, when suddenly we noticed, not too far from our boat, three men in a canoe. They were respectably dressed and when they called to us and asked us if we could tow them along behind us upstream, something impressed me. Something I did not understand led me almost involuntarily to reach out to the throttle and stop the boat.

"Jack," I called to my son, who was then about fifteen years old, "throw them a line." They came alongside and we made the canoe fast. One of the men stayed in the canoe. The other two came aboard our boat and stood with Jessie and Jack and me near the wheel while we talked about the jute crop and the weather and the hazards of the shifting currents. They were friendly and we were having a pleasant chat when suddenly one of them said, "Which side of the rocks are you going on?"

I saw no rocks at all—only the green bank with its lovely Pan Rosa trees off the port side and the gray-yellow water of the Amazon. "What rocks?" I asked.

Without answering, the man grabbed the steering wheel out of my hand and turned it completely around. Our boat wheeled giddily and shot out away from the bank into the river. Then I looked back and saw, not twenty feet in front of where we had been heading, the jagged points of hundreds of rocks just beneath the surface of the water. One second more and we would have plowed into them and ripped our boat to shreds. We had no idea that these rocks were there and without our hitchhiking friends we would have lost our boat and, in all likelihood, our lives.

Our visitors seemed to take our expressions of gratitude almost casually, however; and a few moments after we had passed this dangerous section of the river, one of them said, "Sir, thank you for the ride. If you do not mind stopping here, we'll get out."

It seemed strange, for there were still no houses or any other sign of human habitation to be seen along the banks. But I stopped, and the men climbed into the canoe and pushed off into the current.

"Look out and see where those men go," I said to Jack. "There's no house around here."

It had been only a moment since they had left us. There were no bends in the river. But after scanning the river in all directions, my boy turned to me. "Dad, they've disappeared."

I turned from the wheel in amazement. There were no rocks, no debris, no sign of struggle or overturned canoe, no cry for help. Only the emptiness of the river and the mute green banks a hundred yards away—too far for them to have reached in that time. Yet the three men and their boat were nowhere to be seen.

We have always believed, Jessie and I, that these men, whoever and whatever they were, were sent to us, the protecting angels of Providence. Man's extremity—and sometimes even his ignorance—is God's opportunity. As I turned back to the wheel of my boat that day, words from the book of Saint Matthew rang in my mind: "He shall give his angels charge concerning thee, and in their hands they shall bear thee up, lest at any time thou dash thy foot against a stone."

We have made many hundreds of trips, short and long, on the river since that first one, and covered tens of thousands of miles along the Amazon and its tributaries. Many of them are great rivers in their own right, deep and dark as night, strong streams that overflow vast regions, drowning tiny farms and clearings and bringing death and devastation to these people. But we have never found help missing when we needed it.

It is a world of contrasts, this Amazon world. A world of backwashes and narrow streams, of floating islands, some of them two miles long; of channels not fifty feet wide but deep enough to accommodate ocean liners. Here is Manaus, a great city rising in the middle of the jungle; all around it is an untamed, trackless world where there are no throughways or roads, paved or unpaved, often not even a visible jungle trail. The tangle that reaches out on every side in the Amazon Valley is one vast sea of green shadows across the width of South America, and the river and its tributaries combine into a series of water roads, a real communication network in the day-to-day lives of the river people.

It was these people whom we served in our nearly three decades on the river. They were Brazilian nationals and natives; storekeepers and plantation owners and laborers—workers on the rubber plantations and in the jute and cotton fields. They were men of varied backgrounds and history; Indians of many tribes, some of them highly cultured and others naked and wild, often dangerous and hostile and ready to kill. The jungle is unique in its multiplicity of types, its blend of the civilized and savage. On one hand are the witch doctors with their trances and incantations. On the other, in our clinics and those the government has been setting up along the river, are penicillin and the latest antibiotic drugs. It is a world of straw-roofed huts and grass skirts, blowguns, poisoned arrows, and drums pounding out savage rhythms; it is also a world past which the new luxury liners steam, en route from Europe or North America all the way up the Amazon to Peru.

But it is still, and for many years will remain, the world of the canoe. To these people the canoe is the bicycle of childhood and the young man's sports car. It is the surrey that takes the family to Sabbath service, the car that goes visiting relatives miles away. It is the housewife's shopping cart and the fisherman's smack and the ambulance for the sick and dying who seek help.

To one who has lived even briefly on the river, the sound of the canoe is as familiar and as easily recognized as the whoosh of a car along a city street.

On that long-past night of remembering, as I lay awake in the darkness of our cabin, I heard a sound breaking into the rhythm of the river shadow. It was growing late, somewhere around ten o'clock, I guessed, from the brightness of the moon on the water outside the cabin window. We had long ago finished our work for the day. But the sounds continued, and seemed to come closer. I got out of the bunk, slipped on a shirt, and, with Jessie following, hurried out on deck.

We stood listening in the night. Now we could hear the canoe coming closer, cutting through the water. Soon the little craft shot out of the shadows on the far side of the lake. It came into the silvery brightness of the moon, and we could see its only passenger—a frail, half-naked boy perhaps eleven or twelve years of age.

As the canoe came closer the boy called out, "Do you have any medicine for the fever?"

The youngster in the boat came alongside. We had a light on now, and in its beam we could see that he was shivering. He lifted his hands to pull himself up, but I saw at once that he did not have the strength. I put my arms around him and lifted him up into the boat. His pale, drawn face told us at once that he was a victim of the terrible malaria fever which at that time was ravaging the area.

His name, he told us, was Antonio. He half pointed, with a weak gesture, when I asked where he lived. "I have been three hours paddling," he said, in Portuguese. "I have been trying to reach your boat."

"Where are your father and mother?"

"My father died yesterday," the boy answered. "My mother is home. She is burning up with high fever."

"Do you have any brothers or sisters?"

"They are both dead, my two brothers. They have been dead a week."

While we were talking with the little boy there on the boat, we were opening up our medical supplies and Jessie was preparing a quinine injection for him. Neither of us is a doctor, but Jessie is a trained nurse. Throughout the river world, particularly during our early days, there were almost no doctors for thousands of miles. Thus we served as physicians and surgeons as needed, performing all kinds of medical work from midwifery to amputations, treating every kind of disease found in that area.

As we gave him his injection, the boy looked up with the hint of a smile on his lips. "Antonio," I asked, "how old are you?"

I have never forgotten his answer. "I am ten years old," he said, "and struggling on toward eleven."

I asked him then, "How long have you been ill with this fever?"

"Three months."

"Haven't you had any treatment?"

"Oh, yes, I have been treated." He paused and added, "I have been treating with the witch doctor."

Jessie, on the other side of the little cabin, glanced at the youngster. "Just what did the witch doctor do for you, Antonio?" she inquired.

His eyes were wide and frightened as he gazed up at us, looking from one to the other as though he, too, were aware of the bizarre things he was saying. "The witch doctor shut us up in a hut," he said. "All of us. He burned bits of hair and feathers and leather, the horns of oxen, anything you can imagine almost."

My wife came over and knelt down beside the boy. "What did he say he was doing all this for?" she persisted.

"To drive out the spirits," the boy said, his small voice almost echoing the tone of the incantations. "To smoke out the evil spirits that brought the fever."

"And it didn't work?"

The boy shook his head. "Then, when he couldn't smoke them out, the witch doctor went out into the woods and got a limb from the thorn tree and beat us with that."

The youngster took off his blouse and showed us his back, covered with deep sores from the beating.

We treated these sores on his back and we gave him medicines for himself and for his mother. There was nothing more we could do for him except to let him hurry home as swiftly as he could. We helped him over the side and down into the canoe; heard his words of thanks and saw him pick up his paddle and start out across the path of moonlight. We followed him with our eyes until he disappeared into the dark shadows beyond.

Antonio was going home. Not to what we who grew up in the United States would consider a real home, but to a hut of mud and palm leaves on the riverbank with the jungles behind and around it, a world of wild animals, snakes, and insects—and the anopheles mosquito which transmits the fever from which he was suffering. His was a home of poverty, sickness, suffering, superstition, and too often death.

This was the world to which we came. It was our assignment, as a part of our church mission, to bring these people, insofar as we could, new hope and new faith and new

vision. It was not our purpose to preach to them complicated dogmas they could not understand; nor to terrify
them with imagined torments of hell. We could help them
only with a message of love, the love of God and of Christ
for them, a love that would care for them and reach out
to them, even to this lonely little kid in his canoe.

This was our purpose and our goal.

The purpose burned strong in my mind after the boy had
left, as Jessie and I stood out on the deck in the cool of the
night.

A new vision. A new meaning to life for a thousand or
ten thousand boys like this one who had come to us weak
and half dead himself, with his pitiable little tale of trau-
matic tragedy in a mud-walled house at the river's edge.

"I am ten years old and struggling on toward eleven."

I could still hear the sound of his paddle as his canoe cut
through the moonlight and shadows.

CHAPTER 2

DESTINATION: RIO

IN certain areas along the Amazon River Valley, there are, surprisingly, settlements of Japanese. Most of them came to the river just before the outbreak of World War II; and after Japan lost the war, these people stayed, some going into business in the ever-growing cities of Brazil, others remaining to farm the rich soil along the Amazon. As the early settlers in North America had done three hundred years earlier, some sent back to their homeland for wives; others married native girls. All of them are hard workers; some of the neatest and best cared-for homes along the river bear the stamp of Japanese energy and artistry.

In one of these homes we were permitted once to hold a religious meeting because, although it was not a Christian family, the owner's father-in-law had been an Adventist for many years. Shortly afterward the wife was baptized into our faith. The husband was slower to believe, but he was deeply impressed with the singing at the meeting— so impressed that he learned all the words of "God Will Take Care of You" by heart and liked to sing them in his odd, tinny, broken Portuguese.

On the Amazon island where these Japanese-Brazilians lived, the chief crop, in addition to the usual rice, was jute

19

or hemp. While the river is low, before floodtime, hemp plants grow twelve feet high in three months' time. As the river overflows, the jute is inundated in several feet of water. To harvest the crop, the men—and often women, too—must work waist high in the water, pulling the jute up by the roots, cutting off the roots with a sharp knife, then tying the rest of the plant into bundles and setting these back into the water to soak. In a few weeks the bark or fiber is loose and can be pulled off easily.

Working constantly in the water, they contend with a whole army of slithering dangers. I have seen hundreds of jute workers come out of those sunken fields with blood-sucking leeches an inch and a half long on their legs. They cannot pull off these creatures without breaking off the teeth and causing infection. Limes are the answer. They are carried by all the workers; they have learned that squeezing lime juice on the leeches makes them fall off.

Toiling one morning in his jute fields, the Japanese farmer who had been exposed to Christianity was singing his favorite "God Will Take Care of You" when he felt what he thought was a leech on his leg. He paid no heed but continued to work, singing away happily in his high voice. Suddenly he felt as if something was crawling in his pant leg. Frightened, he ran from the water and snatched off his pants. As he shook them, an eighteen-inch poisonous snake slipped to the ground and slithered away.

There were tears in the man's eyes as he told me the story. "Pastor, I did not know it was there but I am sure that snake would have bitten me and I would have died if I had not been thinking about God and singing that hymn. I believe it. I believe He protected me in that jute field, when I did not know."

Many times Jessie and I have known that same protection and that same guidance. All of our lives, it seems, we have lived in the midst of peril, and never has harm come to us.

Any expedition, whether to climb Mount Everest or to rescue lost souls in the Amazon, is a matter of planning and preparation, on which may ultimately depend triumph or failure, even life or death. It is almost fantastic how much preparation for our Amazon adventure Jessie and I received, without realizing it at all, in a world ten thousand miles away. Nebraska, with its flat outstretching fields of grain and prairie, where my grandmother once placated a band of murder-bent Sioux Indians with nine loaves of her special fresh-baked bread and a litter of newborn puppies, at first thought seems an unlikely spot for which to prepare for a missionary life in the South American jungle.

But they are not so different, after all. Life close to the soil, where nature can be enemy or friend, is closely akin to life on the river. The self-sufficiency I learned as a boy on a Nebraska farm stood me in good stead years later in the Brazilian jungle.

When my father, Sam Halliwell, came out west with his family as a boy of fifteen, Nebraska was still a frontier world, as the Amazon is today. Large herds of buffalo roamed the grass-covered plains. Indians still claimed all the land, and resented fiercely the settlers and the coming of the Union Pacific tracks. Attacks and killings were frequent.

Often Sioux raiding parties would cross the Platte River from the north to burn homes or to lasso the smokestacks of Union Pacific locomotives as the trains chugged by. They hoped to drag these iron horses bodily from the tracks. Some of them, not lucky enough to have their ropes break, were dragged to their death.

Many settlers, driving off these Sioux attackers, paid with their lives. My father's family might easily have met this end, for one night a band of these marauders attacked their home, surrounding the house and screeching threats to burn the place down unless they were let in. Once inside, they stole everything—food, livestock, furniture, farm tools, chickens, even the one gun in the house, which was used only to kill game for food. By the grace of God, the family was spared.

This was the world in which my father grew up and in which, in 1884, he married Mary Rall, daughter of another pioneer family. The fourth oldest of their eight children, I grew up in this same rugged and untamed world, close to the earth. I fished and hunted and rode wild ponies. I skated on the Platte River in the middle of Nebraska's bitterest winters, and plowed my way to school through five-foot snows. Each morning before dawn it was my chore to drive the cows from the corral near our house out to pasture on our farm, a mile from town.

When I was nine it became my job to ride the lead horse on the binder and to keep the animals out of the wheat. The sun would blaze down hot, the day would be long, and sometimes astride the horse I would doze off for an instant. Then I would hear my father's voice shouting above the roar of the binder, "Get out of the wheat, boy— keep them out of the wheat."

Years later I was staying at a plantation on one of the Brevis Islands in the Amazon. The Brazilian owner operated a store, raised all kinds of fruits and vegetables, and ran a small sugar-cane press that was operated by a yoke of oxen. The oxen had to walk around and around all day, and someone had to follow them and keep them going. Usually, I learned, this was the chore of one of the many sons of the owner. Watching one of those sons—a ten-year-old trudging behind the oxen, shouting at them in his high young voice—I thought of the farm and my father and the binder back in Nebraska.

But Brazil was only a large pink spot on the map in 1909 when, at eighteen, I finished high school and embarked on my first real job—teaching in a one-room country school in a tiny settlement in far-off Idaho. In that remote spot, in the midst of the tall pines, with the mountains towering on every side, there came to me what I can only call a vision, almost a command.

The Bear River drains that part of Idaho and flows on down into the Great Salt Lake, twisting and bending and turning back upon itself, a coiling, foaming mass of water that plunges through pass and ravine and gorge. Near the town of Grace, a dam and a great electric power plant had been built, with generators that furnished power and light to Ogden and Salt Lake City.

The idea of being a part of such an operation, helping to bring light and power to whole cities of people, seemed a magnificent way to serve the needs of modern life. As I would stand and listen to the sounds of the generators and the roar of the water, a voice seemed to be crying within me, "You can also do things like this. Prepare. Prepare yourself."

I had no money to study electrical engineering, no previous training, and no connections whatever in this field. Yet this was what I knew I was going to be.

When school was over and I went home, I unfolded

this new dream to my family. Like me, they had more enthusiasm than money; but with what funds we could raise in the family, my meager savings, and what I would be able to earn tending furnace and waiting on tables in a student rooming house, it looked as if I would just be able to make it. While I waited for fall, I took all the odd jobs I could get. One of them, the luckiest, was playing the fiddle at barn dances to pick up a few extra dollars in the evening. I say "lucky," for it was at one of these dances that I noticed a lovely brown-eyed girl in a white dress, her slim waist belted in red. I lost no time finding out who she was, and once I did I handed my fiddle to another member of the orchestra. "Hold this, I'm going to meet that girl."

That was my first dance with Jessie.

I think now that we were certain, almost from our first dance together, to the rhythm of those Nebraska fiddles, that our lives were inextricably bound together. By the time I went off to Lincoln that fall, to enroll at the University of Nebraska, we had made our plans. Neither of us was twenty. Jessie had promised to wait for four years, until I had finished my engineering course and we could marry.

But when I returned to Kearney the following spring, I discovered a subtle but important change in Jessie. She had come upon a religion that caught her interest deeply —the religion of the people who called themselves Seventh-day Adventists.

We had both been brought up in devout families. We had talked about religion and had agreed that ours was to be a Christian home. Together we had visited churches of different faiths to decide which most appealed to us.

Now I realized that she had accepted this faith and was eager for me to want to follow her lead. That summer we began to attend services together. It was not long before I came to realize that this religion and its truth had deep meaning for me, as well as for Jessie.

It was a simple and not particularly earth-shaking event —the fact that two people in love happened to find a faith they wanted to share together.

But of great importance to both of us was the dedication to service we found in this faith. Jessie was enthralled by the remarkable work the Adventists did in the field of medicine, by the hospitals and clinics that had been established in many remote missionary fields throughout the world as well as in the States.

When I returned to my engineering studies at Nebraska University at the end of the summer, Jessie went to Lincoln, too—to begin a three-year nursing course at the Adventist hospital.

How could we have guessed then the role this training would play in our own lives, and in the lives of hundreds of people of whose existence we did not then even dream?

I think of Jessie going out at all hours of the day or night in Brazil's ancient city of Salvador, to help deliver babies in the huddled world of twisting streets. I can see her delivering the afterbirth of a frail, half-dead woman lying on a mud floor in an Amazon straw shack—and thereby saving that woman's life. Jessie delivered hundreds of babies along that river; in every settlement today there are little Brazilian girls who answer to the American name of Jessie.

One family who lived far up the river—about twelve

hundred miles from the mouth—seemed to need her mid-wifery skill every time our boat arrived in that district.

"Isn't it remarkable," Jessie asked the mother once, "that the baby always seems to arrive precisely at the time our boat arrives on our yearly trip up the river?"

"Why no, it isn't particularly remarkable," the woman answered. "We plan it that way."

Civilization had not yet arrived in many communities along the river, but planned parenthood was already in operation.

There were moments of amusement and moments of grim tragedy in that world. Youngsters were brought to us too late to help or to save; adults often put their faith in superstitions and voodoo rituals rather than in the modern medicine that we tried to bring to them.

Yet none of our help would have been possible without the training which began, for Jessie, in that hospital in Lincoln, Nebraska.

In a different way, my training in electricity, my knowl-edge of motors and generators and power circuits, was put to use in our work in Brazil. The boat on which we traveled that network of the Amazon waterways, the thou-sands of meetings we held, showing colored motion pic-tures and providing light and amplifiers so that all could hear above the jungle night—all of this was dependent in large measure on this experience and training in electricity without which we would often have been helpless.

I recall one night when we set up a meeting in a clear-ing close to the water's edge, putting up our own screen and doing all the wiring in a matter of hours so that liter-ally hundreds of natives and nationals were able to hear us and see the pictures of the life of Christ which we showed.

From miles around, the canoes appeared, loaded with passengers who sat quietly in their craft throughout our meeting. It was, I feel certain, the first Amazon drive-in theater.

Power for a prayer meeting, the electrical system for a native clinic, helping to plan the electrical needs of a hospital in Belém, in how many ways did that training help us in our work and our lives! I remember particularly one Brazilian who examined the generator on our boat with great care and then declared, "It is remarkable. You bring all your own power with you—spiritual and electrical as well."

But back in Nebraska, as we worked and studied, we had no idea that our faith was to lead us so far from home.

This church to which we both belong, however, is one which is concerned with remote corners of the world, in the need there, and in sending its members to give Christian service and help to the world's people. Ours was and is a missionary church in its truest sense, the mission of service to others.

We believe that a major part of our "assignment" on earth is bringing help where it is needed. Adventist doctors and nurses, Adventist clinics and hospitals, are found on every continent. In less than a hundred years of missionary activity, our faith has established churches in 185 countries.

Workers within our faith preach in 748 languages and dialects. Our books and tracts are published, sold, or distributed free in 213 languages. The church operates twenty-three sanitariums and hospitals in North America, and eighty-two overseas. The latter alone treat more than 1,500,000 outpatients a year, in addition to 122,000 inpatients. Mission dispensaries and clinics care for more than 800,000 additional patients annually. Ten schools of nursing in North America and twenty-one overseas, graduating a total of more than five hundred nurses a year, help staff these hospitals and clinics. So, too, does the magnificent College of Medical Evangelists, located at Loma Linda, California, and Los Angeles. Founded by the church in 1905 to train medical missionaries, this modern medical center today has three main schools—medicine, nursing, and dentistry—and six related schools for dietetics, tropical and preventive medicine, physical therapy, X-ray technology, medical technology, and graduate studies.

These schools have graduated thousands of doctors and nurses of all religious faiths. As this is written, more than a hundred of these graduate physicians—and more than a hundred of the graduate nurses—are serving overseas in our mission hospitals.

All of this was very real in our minds because it was real to our faith, but our own program and plans were much more immediate and down to earth.

In the summers I took whatever work I could get to help pay my university expenses. Mostly it was on farms and sometimes it was rugged. Sometimes we worked on a threshing machine from farm to farm on a regular schedule. Once I even did my threshing at the point of a gun when an angry farmer insisted on having his work done ahead of the others.

During the school year I continued to tend furnace at a student boardinghouse. In my senior year I worked nights at the Lincoln light plant. And finally, in 1916, the degree was mine. With war raging in Europe, electrical engineers were being offered good jobs. I accepted one with a tractor company in Charles City, Iowa, which was making howitzer mortar shells for the Allies.

Sometimes, in my first weeks on the job, I would stand and watch the scrap iron and steel, old plows, and other farm machinery being dumped into the steel furnaces to be fashioned into shells, and I would remember the words of the prophet Joel, written many centuries ago: "Prepare war, wake up the mighty men, let all the men of war draw near; let them come up: Beat your plowshares into swords, and your pruninghooks into spears; let the weak say, I am strong."

On October 1, 1916, Jessie was graduated from the nursing school in Lincoln. Two days later, on October 3, we were married in Mason City, Iowa, and the following day we began our life together in a humble dwelling in Charles City.

The next year we were in the war, and in that era of turmoil and sacrifice and super-emotionalism, I was ordered to stay on my job as plant electrician because we were turning out vital war materials.

Two weeks before the Armistice, Jessie gave birth to our son. The influenza epidemic was sweeping across the world, claiming millions of lives, and Jessie was terribly ill even as our son was born. We did not know whether she or our son, who was also affected by the disease, would survive. It was a time of tension and anxiety, but we held fast to our faith in His protection, and within a few weeks they were past the danger point and getting well.

Amidst the worry over Jessie and the baby, I didn't

give much thought to the matter of a name for our son. It was not until later that we discovered that the nurse, who was also under considerable strain, had told the doctor the baby was to be called "Claris." By that time it was too late—the name had been officially recorded. But we call our son Jack.

Both Jessie and I had regretted, when we settled down in Charles City, that there was no church of our faith there, but before many months had passed an evangelist arrived. From his meetings developed a permanent organization of which I was chosen leader—and through this had my first experience in conducting services. As time went on, I became more and more interested in my church work and less and less in my job at the plant.

Two books made a deep impression on me: *On the Trail of Livingstone,* written by a missionary about his work in Africa, and *In the Land of the Incas,* the story of a missionary's life in Bolivia and Peru. The achievements of these men in salvaging human souls convinced me that we, too, must play a greater part in this work. You cannot, we felt, work part time for faith.

Jessie and I talked and prayed for days, and at last we knew in our hearts that this was right for us. In the spring of 1920 I applied to our church conference for work on a full-time basis.

The officials were delighted at my decision. They were, of course, uncertain as to what assignment I might receive for overseas service, or when. But there was other work to be done, close at hand.

Within a few weeks we were busy at it. An evangelistic campaign in Cedar Falls, Iowa, came first. We went on from there to Fort Madison, where I supervised the building of a new church while I also had charge of our churches in nearby Burlington and Keokuk.

In the routine of caring for the activities of three churches, and counseling and guiding the people and families of our congregations, the missionary dream was pushed into the background. There seemed hardly time for such wild ideas.

Then one day, late the following summer, the postman handed me a letter from the Mission Board of the Seventh-day Adventists. I called Jessie, so we could open it together.

Our proposal to go to Brazil as missionaries had been under advisement for some months, the letter said, and as the needs in that country had become more and more pressing they had made their decision. We were to make preparations at once and be ready to sail for Rio de Janeiro on the Munson liner *Aeolus,* scheduled to leave from New York on October 15. The sailing date, by an odd coincidence, happened to be my thirtieth birthday.

Our hearts were light and heavy, all at the same time, as we stood on the deck of the *Aeolus* watching the New York skyline fade into the distance. We were sad at leaving our families and our home and our country. But we were happy at the thought that at last we were embarked on the work to which we had been called. The fall wind was cold as we left our homeland but as the days passed the weather became warmer, the sky sunny and bright. It was a lush spring morning when, on October 30, we looked out our porthole and saw the green mass of Cape Frio, our first sight of Brazil.

CHAPTER 3

BAÍA

BRAZIL has heavy rains and high waterfalls, large oysters and frogs and alligators and snakes, and water lilies three feet across. In the lush splendor of the Amazon Valley, anything will grow, although south and west of the valley are dry areas where droughts may last for several years. It is a land where plenty and want often sit side by side.

In its backwoods are small one-street sleeping villages where, remote from modern life, living conditions are so primitive as to be almost unbelievable. Yet there are also great cities, particularly in the south: Rio; São Paulo, the fastest growing city in the world; Manaus, a modern metropolis in the middle of the jungle; and Recife, the Venice of the Western Hemisphere. It is a world of magnificent extremes—flamingoes and factories, great universities and blowguns, ultra sophistication and the fine art of poisoned darts.

Less than five hundred years ago—in 1500—a squadron of thirteen ships set sail from Lisbon, Portugal, with much fanfare, colorful plumage, and gleaming armor, bent on reaching and capturing Calcutta, India, by way of South America's Cape Horn. The ever-prevailing trade winds from the east carried these ships to the coast of a new land, rich and fertile, which was promptly claimed for the Portuguese throne. A later expedition carried back to Portugal a cargo of bright-red wood from this land of so many varieties of wood that to this day the number, reaching into the thousands, has never been fully ascertained. The red dyewood was so bright and glowed so intensely that it seemed almost to be on fire. For this reason it was called *brasso*—meaning a live coal. So did the new land where this wood was found get the name Brazil.

Another expedition from Portugal sailed into Guanabara Bay, far south of the Amazon on the Brazilian coast, on the first of January, 1502. Thinking that this bay, which seemed to go on endlessly—it is actually just over thirty miles long—must be the mouth of a great river, it was promptly called the River of the First of January. From this came the shortened version of the name: Rio de Janeiro.

We sailed into this harbor on October 30, 1921, to begin our new work. It was a magnificent sight. On our right was the beautiful city of Niterói, with its background of many-hued mountains. Just behind us on the other side was the round soaring form of Sugar Loaf Mountain, extending in a great sweeping amphitheater across the entire horizon. Before us was the city of Rio itself, with its white gleaming buildings and its red-tiled roofs, thousands upon thousands of them, in a splashing pattern of color and sunlight and shadow. Of special significance to us was still another mountain, the Corcovado, on top of which stands the towering statue of Christ the Redeemer, arms outstretched, above the city.

Coming into a world we did not know, to begin a life we could not fully foresee, our excitement ran high. It was to be a life of service, but in a new and strange land, where the people spoke a language we did not yet know, where the customs and ideas and ways of doing differed entirely from ours, where almost certainly some people would be hostile to our ideas and beliefs and our teachings. We had to come to help, not to take; to advise and guide and uplift where we could, but not to impose our will, our belief, or our language. We had come only to bring a message of love and to give love in terms of help.

This, I knew in my heart, was the real challenge facing us that sunlit morning, as our steamer, with the mothering tugboats at her sides, edged closer to the dock and what would be, for us, the beginning of a new life.

Momentarily there was the sense of the strange and the different. Where would we begin all of this work, and how? How long would it take us to learn the language, to begin to know enough to be of help? How quickly would we begin all this?

On the dock, as we came in closer, I saw a group of people who apparently had recognized us and were waving at us. One of them had in his hand a copy of one of our Adventist magazines. It was like a touch of home to Jessie and me.

Coming into any new city is always something of an adventure, and arriving in Rio this is particularly true, for it is one of the most exciting and beautiful cities in the world.

When I think back on our arrival there, I always recall another occasion when we came into Rio, years later, under far different circumstances. My wife and I were flying in from the Amazon then with a tribal chief who had never before been out of the jungle.

How full of wonder he was! Soon after we took off, we were flying over the jungles at about ten thousand feet and, instead of the steaming heat the chieftain was used to in the half-naked world below, it was suddenly very cold. His lips were blue and he was shivering under his blanket. But as he looked out the window, he could see the bright sun. Puzzled, he said to my wife, "Why is it that we are so high and so near the sun, but it is so cold up here?"

And we tried to explain *that* to a man who still hunted with a war club!

The chief had been staying in one of our hospitals in the north of Brazil for about two weeks waiting for this trip, and he had not particularly enjoyed the vegetarian diet he shared there with us. On this flight the plane came down at the city of Goiana for dinner. When a big thick steak was served to the chief, somehow he did not get a knife or fork. I started to call the waiter, but the chief stopped me. "No, no—I do not need those things. I would prefer to use my hands." Which he promptly did.

When we arrived in Rio that night, there were more than a score of reporters and television people waiting to meet our charge and interview him. They were full of questions about what he thought of this modern world into which he had been transported overnight. What was the most extraordinary thing he had encountered so far, they asked. The old chief grinned: "That big thick steak they gave me to eat last night."

But at the convention of young church people, when someone asked him why he had not brought along his arrows and darts and other Indian paraphernalia, the answer of this aged tribal leader to his young questioner was, "I am no longer an Indian but a Christian."

Our own arrival in Rio was perhaps not so vast a contrast as that the tribal chief experienced when he finally saw the streets and buildings of Brazil's capital and major seaport; yet it was, for us, as for any tourist, new and strange, beautiful and exciting. We were in a world where most people did not speak or understand our language—a world of brilliant sun, tropical trees, and wide sidewalks with dazzling mosaic designs; a magic place that seemed to capture the imagination as no other city does.

But our enjoyment of the vistas of Rio and the magic charm of the city was momentary. We were not tourists on a pleasure cruise; we were here on business. Only a few days after our arrival, church officials gave me my travel orders: We were to proceed at once to a city called Salvador in the state of Baía, seven hundred and fifty miles to the north along the coast of Brazil. In Salvador I was to take over as director of the newly set-up Baía Mission of our church.

We had barely heard of Salvador, but in that ancient city no one had heard of us and only a handful of souls knew about the Seventh-day Adventists and their presence in the Brazilian state of Baía.

Much of the district of Baía is farmland. Its crops are lemons and oranges and every kind of citrus fruit, as well as tobacco, sugar, and cotton. It produces cattle and hogs and poultry, and nearly a hundred different kinds of beans —no other place in the world has as many different kinds of beans as Baía. From the earth come, too, iron and manganese and oil, and black diamonds for commercial uses.

Yet, for all this activity, much of the state is wild, subtropical, and sparsely populated; and across the wide flat areas of farmland are many drought-parched districts with widely scattered one-street towns where a handful of houses huddle under the blazing Brazilian sun.

In all these towns, without fail, can be seen the high gleaming spire of the Catholic church or cathedral, some dating back hundreds of years. Originally Roman Catholicism was the official religion of Brazil and it remained so for many centuries, until the establishment of the Republic in 1889. Today all religions are equal in that country and work in amity for their congregations. But the *padres,* hard working as they may be, are still limited in number in the remote areas, and the communities each priest must serve are widely scattered. In many instances these churches, with their lofty spires, can be fully used—or used at all—only on those occasions when a priest is able to reach them.

Many of the people in these areas had fallen away from their faith, or had grown up with little or none. Their lives were as desolate and hopeless and seemingly purposeless as the parched, somnolent little towns themselves. It was to help these people to find a new meaning and purpose in their lives that we had been sent to Baía.

Salvador itself, which was to be our headquarters, is an ancient port city, once the capital of Brazil. It is built on two levels connected by two modern elevators and, for those who prefer to walk, an ancient flight of four hundred steps. The full name of the city, in Portuguese, is São Salvador de Baía de Todos os Santos—Saint Saviour of the Bay of All Saints. But most people speak of the city and the state interchangeably as Baía.

The lower part of the city is the area of commerce and shipping. There, among the coffee and sugar firms and the great buildings where the cacao is stored, the air is a blend of smells—from the harbor, the coffee and tobacco, the bananas and sugar cane. In the harbor itself are hundreds of small fishing boats anchored alongside large ships and liners, some Brazilian, others flying foreign flags.

Baía is an ancient town still and in the high city, where most of the people live, the old cobblestone streets are narrow and steep. In the days when we arrived and, in fact, until quite recently, there were hundreds of mule carts on these streets. All of them had steel-rimmed wheels, and we could see the sparks fly as they struck the cobblestones.

To us, it was a fascinating city we had come to, a city of legend and culture and history. It had grown rich on sugar and the slave trade, until slavery was abolished in the late nineteenth century, and some of the wealth had gone into its many beautiful churches. There are 365 of them, a church for every day of the year. Many of the buildings are faced with the brilliant-blue tiles which Brazilians call *azulejos*. There have been improvements in Baía since the days when we first arrived; many of the streets in the high city are now new and wide and paved with modern macadam or cement, and there are modern stores and buildings.

But in the days when we arrived the city was still lazing sleepily in its lovely if slightly frayed ancestral dress. We had no time to laze with it. First we had to find living quarters and then set about the organizing work of the mission. There was little money for our personal expenses; our income from the church amounted to only a few dollars a month at that time. We finally had to settle for an apartment on the second floor of a narrow old building on one of those steep, narrow cobblestone streets. There were people above us, below us, and on all sides of us. They were people whose language we did not know, whose customs were strange to us. The apartment was moldy and dark. But it was—at last—the real beginning of our work.

In that beginning, we were close to our own church people, of course, as we launched into the job of organizing and building and expanding our church activity.

One of our happiest meetings was with the Storches—Pastor Gustavo Storch, his wife, and the two-week-old baby on the satin cushion whom we saw at our first Sabbath service in Brazil. In Baía, and later on the Amazon, they were to become our good friends. Pastor Storch was one of the valiant workers of our church and he played a large role in our missionary activity in the Amazon Valley.

At the same time we were trying to adjust ourselves to this new world, its people and its ways. Not far from us was a kindly Catholic woman who spoke some English. She became our friend and taught us our first Portuguese. She was a good teacher and a wonderful human being.

Those early weeks and months were a time of trial— and some amusement as well. As we began to meet native families, we discovered that many of them knew as little about the United States of America as our people did about the United States of Brazil. One night, not long after we arrived in Baía, a Brazilian Army lieutenant and his wife came in to see us.

We had an enjoyable if somewhat difficult time trying out the Portuguese which we were so anxious to learn, and which today we speak as fluently as our native English. Finally the lieutenant's wife asked Jessie, "Where are you people from?"

"We're from the United States," Jessie said.

The woman looked puzzled. "United States? Where is that? Does it belong to Brazil?"

The lieutenant told her quickly, "Wife, don't be foolish. Everybody knows the United States is a part of England."

We laughed, but every day we were impressed with our own ignorance. Even to go to the open market—where it seemed that everything under the sun was sold—presented serious problems in the first days. We did not know the food or the language or how much anything cost. We didn't even know too well the values of the various coins and bills.

We would go to the market, point to the things we wanted, and hold out a handful of coins in payment. The merchant would take out the amount required, and in only a few cases did one take more than the proper sum. But we soon learned the proper evaluations for ourselves, for our wages were limited and every milreis had to count.

Our funds did stretch to include a maid-of-all-work, who was more than worth the infinitesimal pay she received.

Tubusa helped us learn the language and acquainted us with the native dishes. Jessie had always been a wonderful cook, but the Brazilian dishes were very different from those she had cooked back in Nebraska. Unlike Tubusa, she didn't know a hundred ways to fix coconut. Most of the dishes had to be prepared from scratch; there were few manufactured foods such as we now find in a supermarket here in the United States. Tubusa thought perhaps we might be disturbed about her cooking for us. Shortly after she went to work for us—a picture out of a storybook, with her bright bandanna and her full wide skirts—she said to us, "You need never worry about my cooking for you. My hands may be black, but they are always clean."

Since we had given her no hint of concern, nor did we have any, we had no idea why she felt impelled to make this remark.

It is the belief of our church—and one with which Jessie and I are in complete agreement, as I mentioned—that it is not the role of a missionary in a foreign land to impose his culture on the people he has been sent to serve. Our job, as we saw it, was first of all to make friends, and Jessie's method was to become acquainted with the women of Baía on a level on which, even with a language barrier, they could meet.

The women of every social stratum lived on a far different level than those in the United States at the time we first arrived. A wife was so protected from the world that she could not even go downtown to buy her own shoes. Her husband would buy them and take them home to her.

A wife would not know—and in most cases still does not —how much money her husband earns. Today, particularly in the southern cities of Brazil, women are far more emancipated than they were twenty-five years ago, but they are still many years behind the women of the United States in the matter of equality.

Jessie's freedom was to them startling. But through our meetings and evenings with these ladies, especially in connection with our church work, Jessie was making friends as she was learning the cooking methods of Brazil. One day she was to be as expert in Brazilian dishes as any native of that country—and accepted by the women as one of them.

One dish that both Jessie and I missed was simple old-fashioned American pie, apple pie particularly. It's strange how much you miss one special dish after a time; it becomes a kind of symbol of the world you have left. We decided finally that perhaps we could teach the women of Baía how to make an apple pie—or a lemon meringue—provided we had the pie tins, a cooking utensil of which they had never heard.

"There must be a tinner in town," I told Jessie. "I'll explain the situation and get him to make us some pie tins."

I found the tinner all right, and he did make us the tins. Jessie baked her first batch of American-style pies with high hopes of showing the Brazilian ladies of Baía a sample of typical American homemade pie. But pride goeth before a fall—and so did the pie tins. The tinner had soldered the bottoms on and the solder had, of course, melted under the intense oven heat. The pie tins had no bottoms, and the pies themselves were ruined.

Later, we sent to America for some real pie tins. Pie—and a number of other American dishes—is known today in many parts of Baía and other sections of Brazil, thanks primarily to Jessie's cooking skill.

But these first weeks were not easy. We were constantly strapped for funds, and so was our mission. To augment resources, Jessie decided she could pick up at least a few cents as a midwife, and be a real help to the community, too. Since many folk in Baía were poor, they used doctors and hospitals as little as they could. (Public-health conditions in Baía and throughout the nation have greatly improved as a result of both governmental and private educational and medical programs.)

Calls began to come in, often late at night. Would Dona

Jessie go to the house at the corner of such and such a street, to help a woman already beginning her labor? And Jessie would hurry off to this house—or, if it were late, we would go together—to bring a child into the world. Sometimes there would be a doctor and sometimes not. For this service the new parents paid her if and as they could; it might be fifty cents in one case, a dollar in another. Often it was nothing.

However, we do not go into this work to amass personal wealth, but to give service. It is the belief of our church that as much as possible of its funds should be used directly for the people and the work for which these funds were given, and that the actual salaries of workers engaged in carrying out this program should be kept to a minimum.

It is a plan with which both Jessie and I are in complete accord. But at that time, in that small apartment looking out on an almost medieval cobblestone street in Baía, trying to organize this new mission and begin the expanding program, trying to pay the rent and feed and clothe ourselves and our three-year-old son, it was without question a grim and difficult challenge.

We had been in the apartment only about two months when Jessie awakened me one night to tell me that our son was crying and apparently ill. "He must have a terribly high fever," she said. "I'm taking his temperature. He's shivering, and he says his head hurts."

She looked at me in concern as she handed me the thermometer. Jack's temperature was just over a hundred and four degrees!

For a moment we were no longer missionaries, we were frightened parents with a sick baby in the middle of the night. We were strangers, here in a strange land, with little idea of how or where to go for help.

Neither of us was speaking much Portuguese yet— we didn't know where we could reach a British or American doctor quickly.

Jessie collected herself first and began using some of the methods for bringing down fever that she had learned in her nurse's training. None of them worked. Hot and cold compresses seemed only to make the fever worse. Whatever disease Jack had, it didn't respond to hydrotherapy.

In my halting Portuguese I tried to get a doctor, but phone connections were not clear, service was not as efficient as it is today, and if the operator understood what I was trying to say, I couldn't comprehend her answer.

Our son's fever was higher now. His body was still shivering, and sweat was pouring from his forehead. We felt alone and cut off from the world by our own ignorance of the language and the people. We could not, in this moment of immediate need, reach them or make them understand. I looked at Jessie. Her head was bowed and I saw that she, as I, was praying to the only source of help we knew.

CHAPTER 4

OXCARTS AND TIGERS

WE sat up with our son all that night. With the first streaks of dawn I set out across the cobblestones to find a doctor. I wanted one I could trust and if possible one who spoke English, so that I could at least talk to him. The first person I reached was the Catholic lady who was teaching us Portuguese, and with her help it wasn't more than an hour before I had found an American physician. He had lived in Brazil for many years and was delighted, he said, to be of service to an American missionary family. On the way back to our apartment, I told him Jack's symptoms. Dr. Downing nodded. "Well, let's hope I'm right and it will not be so bad. Let us hope I'm right."

Jack's fever was still high when we reached the apartment and the doctor made his examination. Finally he looked up with a smile and said softly, "It is not bad because we have reached him in time. Your son has malaria."

"How serious an attack is it?" Jessie asked, in a tone of quite non-professional, motherly alarm.

"Well, rather severe, I'd say, but not *too* severe." The physician answered her quietly, and his calmness was a tonic to us. In those days there was only one known remedy for malaria—quinine, which is terribly bitter and difficult to give a child who cannot swallow a big capsule.

"Don't worry," Dr. Downing said, looking up at us from the side of the bed. "We'll have him fixed up with a chocolate syrup that tastes like an American ice-cream soda, and he'll never know there's quinine in it. In a few days he'll be perfectly well."

"Will there be other attacks?" my wife asked.

I knew she was thinking of moments when we might be in remote areas, under conditions that would be far more difficult than the capital of Baía presented.

He shrugged. "There is always that danger, of course. Anywhere you go in a tropical zone there is that danger. As long as you have quinine available, however, you can always bring it under control. And there is no reason for a recurrence, actually, unless—"

Both Jessie and I knew enough about malaria to realize that it is transmitted by one special type of mosquito—the female anopheles, known in some areas as "the deadly ladies of the night," because they strike only after darkness. But we had thought we were protected as long as we kept ourselves fully covered whenever we went out after dark.

The doctor, however, was looking around at our apartment. Then he turned back to us. "For your safety and your son's, you will have to get out of this place at once."

To our unasked questions, he went on to explain: "Old buildings like this are infested with malaria mosquitoes; they breed in the walls and cracks in the rotting plaster. That means your son will be reinfected, and each time the attacks will be more severe."

We must move to some place near the ocean, where the air would be largely mosquito free, he told us. Otherwise,

he added quietly, we would have to give up our whole
missionary dream and return to the United States.

Finding new living quarters, in a matter of days at most,
seemed at first an insurmountable problem. We knew
neither where nor how to look. But whenever there is a
need, there is only one main Source of supply, and it is
always our policy at prayers each morning and each night
before retiring to ask His help and to have confidence that
this help will come.

In this case, despite the difficulties which beset us, we
found what we wanted, a lovely house outside the city
itself, overlooking the beach and the ocean—at a price that
was within our limited financial reach.

Jack's malaria vanished almost at once and did not come
back. And we were happy as larks in our charming house,
with its exhilarating panorama of sea and sand and sun
and the ocean winds that cooled the tropical nights.

Tubusa, our *mãe preta*, moved with us, of course.

In the midst of our personal problems, we had not lost
sight of the work we had come to do. Our church group
in Baía was expanding, and we were already planning to
start forays into the backwoods regions and farmlands.
We decided first to follow our "colporteurs," or book salesmen, who had already started at least some interest in
Adventist literature and beliefs in the more remote areas
of the territory. One trip we planned was a lengthy and
difficult journey up the San Francisco River to a community far back in the hinterlands. Most of it would have
to be made on horseback, muleback, or by canoe.

I delayed leaving for this work, however, because Jessie
was pregnant. She herself wasn't worried, but I refused
to leave until our second child was born. Marian, as we

called our daughter, arrived on August 22, 1922, less than a year after we had reached Brazil. She has always been "our little Brazilian"—and although she is an American citizen she can also, if she wishes, claim citizenship in the land of her birth.

Shortly after her arrival, I left my little family in the care of Tubusa, and started on this long-postponed but important evangelistic journey to a remote and inaccessible area hundreds of miles in the interior.

One of the reasons for the trip was a request for help which had reached us by letter from a group of people living far out on the banks of the Corrente River, in the southwest corner of the state of Baía. What they had heard of the simple directness of our faith appealed to them. Could we send an evangelist to teach them?

So we started out. Since I did not yet speak the language well, I took with me one of my co-workers in Brazil, Gustavo Storch, to serve as my interpreter and assistant.

From Baía we traveled for two days by train across the state, through flat, treeless, bleak farmland. The locomotive burned wood, and as we chugged along, black smoke poured out of its stack and sparks flew regularly in every direction. We had been warned to wear old clothes and we were glad we had heeded the advice. Our good clothes would have been ruined by the smoke if they weren't already burned by the embers.

It was with a sigh of relief that we arrived, two days later, at the tropical river-port village of Juaziro, which lies on the banks of the San Francisco River. Here, while we waited for the steamer which was to take us up the stream to its junction with the smaller Corrente, we spent most of our time trying to get the cinders and the smell of smoke out of our clothes and hair.

The boat was a curious vessel, long and wide and as tall as a three-story house, not too different from the river boats which plied the Mississippi in the middle of the nineteenth century. It was propelled by a wheel on the stern which splattered water in every direction.

The San Francisco is one of the few large rivers of the world that flow north, so we were heading south as we made our way slowly upstream, stopping at almost every village along the way. There was little refrigeration on board and no place to keep fresh meat in that hot humid world. Every day or so a new steer, purchased at one of the villages on our way, was slaughtered for our food. The drinking water was simply dipped out of the river but was neither filtered nor boiled.

It took us nineteen days on this boat to reach the Corrente. Two days more by a little boat and, thirty days after we had set out, we arrived at Pôrto Velho, the community which had asked for our help.

The village—the name means Old Port—consisted of only a scattering of houses, many with palm-thatched roofs and bare mud walls. But the people seemed delighted that we had come. We agreed to hold a series of meetings for them, and to tell them the meaning of the love of Christ for them and for all people everywhere.

This was always the first message that we tried to bring to people—that they should put their trust in God and in Christ as the Son of God and in the Word of the Bible itself. Our message is one of love, not fear; of forgiveness for the repentant, not despair or brimstone.

It was this message of joy, with its many ramifications

and responsibilities, religiously and socially and morally, that we were here to bring to this group, and we agreed to stay with them for two weeks.

Our first meeting started out well. We had found a large room to serve as a meeting hall and in its center had set up a powerful kerosene pressure lamp to provide light. By meeting time the hall was crowded with men and women—some Indians but most of them Brazilian nationals who were largely of Portuguese extraction. Suddenly, as we were about to announce the opening hymn, one of the women screamed, jumped up, and ran down the improvised aisle and out of the building.

"I don't know what's the matter," my assistant said to me under his breath. "Shall we stop the meeting to find out?"

"We'd better try to keep going as planned," I suggested.

But before we could get our hymn started several other women had jumped up and run out, and soon they were streaming out in droves. The reason—when we discovered it—was incredible: frogs, not by hundreds but by thousands, had invaded our meeting place and were leaping off the walls and over the seats trying to get to that powerful kerosene lamp by which we were lighting the hall!

It was a real invasion. The frogs, two or three inches long, were coming from every direction and leaping over anything that stood in their path. Some climbed high on the walls and then attempted a broad jump in the direction of the light, only to land on a woman's hair or skid down the back of her neck. Pioneer women many of them were, used to primitive conditions, but to frogs they

Parade of the *Luzeiros* coming to port for supplies.

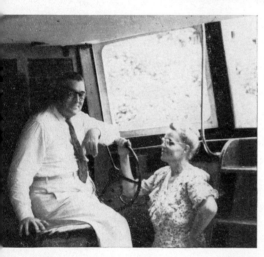

Missions Picture,
General Conference of
Seventh-day Adventists
Jessie and I aboard the *Luzeiro*.

Missions Picture
People along the Amazon are frequently flooded out of their homes. Here the *Luzeiro* brings assistance.

A native dwelling on the Amazon.

Native craft on the Amazon.

Visitors come to welcome the *Luzeiro*.

Jessie at work on board the *Luzeiro*.

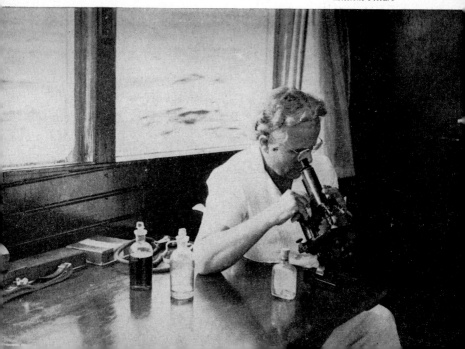

Jessie and I and patients.

This woman is getting her first injection. She is standing in a canoe alongside the *Luzeiro* while Jessie gives her the injection through the window.

Missions Picture

Jessie holding clinic at one of the regular stops of the *Luzeiro*.

A baptism in the Amazon.

An Indian from the Araguay River tribe called Caraja. The rings under his eyes are the tribal mark of the Carajas.

A Caraja chief and his wife with their five-month-old grandchild.

Missions Picture

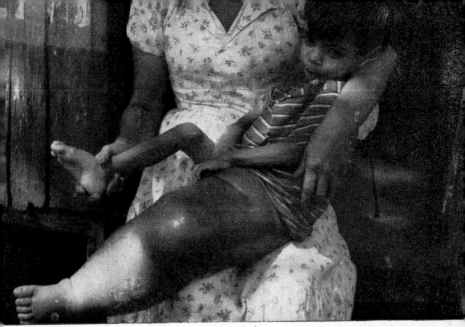

Missions Picture

Elephantiasis, a condition we often found among the people of the Amazon.

Jessie examining a patient.

Missions Picture

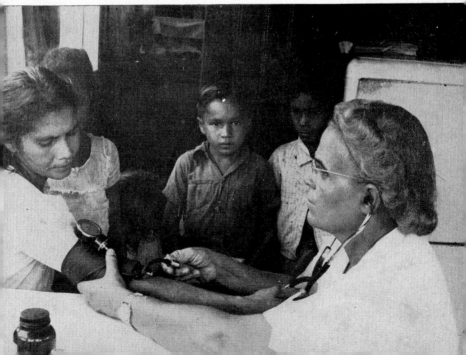

Jessie at the wheel of the *Luzeiro*.

Fishing along the Amazon pays big dividends.

reacted just as the members of the ladies' aid back home would react to mice.

Our first meeting, which we'd had pretty well organized, we thought, wound up a shambles. But we had learned, as we were constantly doing. By meeting time next night we had the frog problem licked—with draperies across the windows.

We stayed for two weeks in the little village of Pôrto Velho, telling the people about our beliefs, our program of service through schools, hospitals, and medical care. Before we left, we had the nucleus of a new church group organized and under way.

We began our most serious work often in the midst of a comedy of errors. We had arranged our return trip so that we would get back to the San Francisco River in time to catch the big river steamer on its return trip. Our timing, I guess, was just a shade too good. The ship was already in port when we arrived. I climbed on board, but my assistant, who had a badly sunburned arm, stopped a moment at a drugstore for some vaseline. By the time he reached the dock, the ship was pulling out into the stream. I hurried to the captain to tell him my companion had been left behind and to ask if the boat could possibly stop and pick him up.

That's what I meant to say, at any rate. But in my excitement, and with my poor Portuguese, I used the wrong gender. To the captain, I was saying that my lady companion had been left standing on the dock.

The captain smiled, a wide understanding smile, pulled a cord, and shouted an order. The ship stopped, the mighty stern wheel went into a reverse spin, spraying tons of water on the decks, and we backed up to the dock to take on my assistant.

When the captain saw who it was he had backed up for, he was decidedly put out. "I thought he said his girl friend," the captain told my assistant later. "If I had known it was a man, I would have let you rot on that deck."

My bad Portuguese had at least kept my friend from a long sun-baked wait.

On my second trip up the San Francisco, not long thereafter, I went alone. I went in answer to an invitation from another group of people who had heard of our work and were interested in it. They lived in a region even farther in the interior, many miles beyond where we had preached before. There were no roads, no river transportation, and the only way to reach this place after we left the river itself was overland on horseback, along trails through the tropical rain forest.

Riding horseback was nothing new to me after my Nebraska upbringing, but the Brazilian saddle, which is like the English saddle in the United States, was new to me and difficult. For this part of the journey I had hired a guide and, since there were two other men going to the same remote community for other purposes, we were a party of four. Because we did not wish to delay our journey, we were traveling at night.

We had not gone far into the woods when my guide gave a warning. I had studied my Portuguese hard in the previous weeks and understood him completely: We were to stay close together as he had seen two jaguars—Brazilian tigers—following us.

The tigers were on the far side of the clearing just behind us, he said.

"I'd like to get a shot at one of those overgrown cats," one of the two strangers told the guide. "When we get to another clearing, you stop on the other side and when those tigers show themselves I'll let one of them have it."

"We will all be torn to shreds if you try it," the guide said quietly.

"Why? Are those tigers stronger than my bullets?"

"There are two of them—that means they are probably mates," the experienced guide explained patiently. "They probably have their young hidden somewhere nearby in the woods. That is why they are following us—they are protecting their young."

"But I don't see—"

"If you shot the female, the male would attack in the smoke of your shot. You leave them alone. They'll stop following us after a while, when they decide the danger is past. They are smarter about that sometimes than humans."

The stranger put away his revolver and we rode on. We did not see the tigers again.

I reached my destination and for a few days was immersed in holding meetings. As I got ready to leave, elated that the Lord had prospered my work, I learned that two men from the village were planning a trip at the same time. Not anxious to start out alone, I arranged with them to take me overland and then by canoe down to where I could catch a San Francisco River steamer.

At that time of the month the moon was full, and the two men suggested that it would be better if we traveled by night when we reached the stream instead of by day when the sun was so hot. They were complete strangers to me and I wasn't eager to travel alone with them at night, but their plan sounded sensible and I agreed.

So we set out at night, the three of us, down the stream, in a small canoe. I sat in the center, with one man at either end of the craft. It was a beautiful night. The full moon shone bright, and the little stream was like a narrow silver ribbon.

We hadn't gone far when one of the men drew out a loaded revolver and put it on the suitcase before him. Then he drew out a knife. "Mister," he called to me across the canoe, "are you armed?"

In all my travels I have never carried a gun or a weapon of any kind. Now I hesitated for a moment, not sure how to answer him, and then I remembered that I had my Bible in my pocket. Paul mentions in his letter to the Ephesians that the sword of the spirit is the Word of God. "Yes," I answered, "I am armed."

He appeared slightly startled but made no reply. We continued on downstream. Soon, however, the moon that had been providing us with light began to disappear under thick dark clouds. There were so many logs in the stream that our journey was hazardous even in the moonlight but now, with this light gone, traveling became almost impossible. At least this was what one of the men told me. We would have to pull into the bank and make an improvised camp for the night, he said. I didn't much like the idea, but apparently I had no choice.

The bank of the stream was high and muddy. As we came close, the man in the front of the canoe did a strange and—as it proved—utterly foolish thing. There was a pole in the canoe and he picked it up, stuck it into the mud of the bank, and literally pole-vaulted to land.

The whole thing happened so quickly that I had no time even to try to warn him that this was dangerous. I saw his dark form swing past me out of the canoe toward the bank and as he struck the ground I heard a shot and a terrible cry of pain. The other man cried out, "Bandits— we've landed in the midst of a bunch of bandits. You'd better get out your gun now, and get out of this boat."

But I hesitated to make my move yet, and so did he. We sat in the canoe for an instant and heard nothing more. Then we edged our boat in closer and leapt out onto the bank. We found our companion a few feet away, lying half in the mud. He was conscious, and told us he had been shot through the foot.

We had landed, actually, not in a bandit's hideout but in a spot where animals—deer and tiger and tapir—came down from the forest to drink. A hunter had set his snare so that an animal would be shot when he tripped the string across the path. He had caught a man instead, who now lay bleeding on the ground.

We had not yet begun our medical missionary work, but the question of what to do for the injured man was immediate. I had no medicine with me except iodine and aspirin tablets. I knew enough, at least, to give him first aid. I tore up one of my white shirts and made bandages, dosed the wound with iodine and bound it up the best I could. Together the other man and I made a bed on the ground and put the wounded man on it.

As we were in woods where we knew jaguars were plentiful, we were afraid at first to go to sleep. Then I recalled that I had with me in my belongings the pressure kerosene lamp that I used for my meetings. We got out the lamp and lit it, and with that light were able to collect enough wood to light a fire. This, I reasoned, would keep away the tigers and give us a chance for a little rest.

But as we dozed off the wounded man began to moan with pain. I got up and went over to him and discovered that an army of black ants, evidently attracted by the blood, had swarmed over his injured foot. Some had even gotten under the bandage and begun to eat the lacerated flesh. I got the man under a mosquito-net covering, put on a fresh bandage, and finally got my folding cot out of the canoe and put him on that, so that the ants could not get at him again.

At last it was dawn! We got the injured man back into the canoe and on down the river to the village where I was to get the steamer. Here we found a pharmacist, who was able to remove the shot and clean the wound. The iodine I had put on it the night before, he said, had helped to prevent infection. My first patient would be all right.

Later that day, while I waited for the river steamer, some of the people who had heard what had happened told me how close I had come to death. Both my traveling companions were known as exceedingly dubious characters; the police of this village wouldn't even allow them to stay in town. I was inclined to believe them, since they also told me that people used to the river, as these two men were, could travel it under all circumstances, day or night.

"They were going into that embankment for one purpose —to kill you, rob you, and leave you for the tigers to dispose of," one man explained succinctly. "You were exceedingly fortunate that they picked that particular spot, and that the first man tripped over the snare."

I thought of the words I have read so many hundreds of times in the Book of Psalms: "The Angel of the Lord

encampeth around about those that fear him and deliv-
ereth them."

Communications in those areas at that time were sketchy
when they weren't just non-existent and there was no way
I could get word back to Jessie. On my first trip to the
Corrente I was gone about two months and she had no
word from me from the time I left the river steamer, which
did carry mail.

On my arrival back, however, I was naturally excited
and happy at the prospect of seeing my family again, but
as I neared the house I smelled medicine. Someone must
be ill! I hurried inside and found Jessie in bed, recovering
from a severe attack of intestinal influenza.

Tubusa had stood by her like a guardian angel when the
attack came, Jessie told me, and had gone for the American
physician, Dr. Downing. The church ladies had come in,
too, to help take care of Jack and baby Marian, although
our house was a long way from the city. And a wonderful
Catholic lady across the street, who had sort of taken us
under her wing, had also helped out in this unhappy time.

Jessie also had one small story, one that I will never forget, about our boy Jack, who was then just four and a half.

One Sunday morning, she said, he had been playing outside the house with some little native boys. He had taken
all his playthings out with him, and although they were
simple toys, to the Baían children they must have seemed
irresistible.

"I was inside reading at the front window and I called
Jack in for something. The other boys were out there beating his drum," Jessie said. "All at once I noticed there was

no more noise. We looked out and found that they had gone, taking all his toys with them."

Jessie felt particularly bad because she had called Jack in and given them the chance to take the things and run off with them into the woods. But our four-and-a-half-year-old boy had a suggestion. "Mother," he said, "if we just had a prayer, I think the boys will bring them back." So they prayed about this together.

The next morning a big Negro lady knocked on our front door. She was holding out her apron—and in it were all Jack's toys. She told my wife, "You know, when that boy came back to my house yesterday—he has no parents and I am taking care of him—he had all these toys and I asked him, 'Where did you get them?' Well, he said, 'An American boy gave them to me.' But I knew that wasn't true. I knew he took them."

The woman said she had tried to get the boy to bring them back himself, but he wouldn't do it. "So I made him tell me the direction of the house and I brought them back myself."

Shortly after my return to Baía from my second trip, I learned some disturbing news. Our doctor informed us that Tubusa, whom we all loved so much, and whom we regarded almost as a member of the family, had been ill for many years with elephantiasis.

We were greatly distressed and asked him if there were some way we could help her. His concern, he explained, was not only for her but also for us, and above all for our children.

Elephantiasis, he explained, is transmitted by the culex mosquito from the infected person to other people in the area. With Tubusa in the house, it was likely that we would all be infected.

Elephantiasis is one of the terrible diseases for which there is no known cure. It doesn't kill, but the leg swells up to two or three times its normal size. Sometimes doctors amputate, but in recent years they have learned to extract the small wormlike creatures which get into the lymph gland and cause this frightful illness. The operation does not cure but it does help.

However, not even this much was known on the day Dr. Downing warned us we must get rid of Tubusa. We protested, for we had come to depend on Tubusa and we did not like the idea of casting her out as the lepers of another day had been treated.

"It is one thing to be religious," the doctor said sternly, "but does your religion give you the right to act foolishly or to take foolish chances? That is what you are doing now, not only for yourselves, but for your two young children."

There was nothing to do but follow his advice. We were more accustomed to giving advice than to taking it. People came to us constantly for help, and we were amazed that many of them, troubled, concerned, anxious for something to hold on to in their lives, had no religion at all. At best it was a mixture of religion and superstition carried over from ancient ways and legends.

Instinctively these people were seeking solid ground on which to build the inner life of faith by which they could, as the Bible tells us, "be born again."

Our work was directed and financed by the Baía Mission of our church, operating under its East Brazil Union. Our church is organized into five unions in South America, and under these unions are subdivisions which we call missions until they are fully organized into conferences. The primary task, of course, is the evangelistic—to build groups and churches on the local level. The medical work, the social work, the schools—all this follows. It was particularly important that we organize schools in Baía because throughout Brazil school is held on Saturday, and for families converted to our faith this made a problem: the children of our faith would not be able to attend school on Saturday, the day we keep sacred for worship.

Throughout this state, scores of groups began to form and churches began to be built, not only in the big cities but even in smaller communities, too. Schools were started. A wave of enthusiasm spread across Baía in the wake of our endeavors.

We had not yet launched our medical missionary work. In the interior of the country, although there is considerable hookworm, there is not the amount of disease found farther to the north, in the hotter jungle areas. Baía is not tropical but subtropical. There are, however, the terrible droughts which afflict this section, particularly in the western part of the state. In some places where we went there had not been a drop of rain for more than four years. In some districts the government had to evacuate the people because the wells and springs and streams and rivers dried up and there wasn't water even for the people to drink.

Because of these dry spells much of the state is treeless and sun-baked. In a typical Baía town you find no trees, and the unpaved streets are sandy. There are more motor vehicles today, and a few jeeps, but in those early days there were practically none. For carrying heavy loads there were only the oxcarts—which are, of course, still widely in use.

These oxcarts are a clamorsome remnant of Baía's primitive past. The wheels are of solid wood, turning on thick axles, and often the carts are so heavy that it takes five yoke of oxen to pull them. These are carts that carry the produce to market—bananas and lemons and cotton and tobacco and all the other colorful fruits and agricultural products of this subtropical soil. They carry the supplies and do much of the toting of materials around the farms and *fazendas,* as the big plantations are called.

The wheels and axles make a terrific clamor, an almost continuous groaning and whining that has a peculiar penetrating quality, like an infant's cry. Riding through the farm areas, we could hear the oxcarts and the strange music of their wheels and axles on every side, a fretful, persistent, yet curiously beguiling clatter in the parching heat of a Baía afternoon.

These backwood regions, lying just south of the full tropical jungle of the Amazon Valley, were and in large measure remain primitive. Most of the houses are built of poles stuck into the ground to which strips of wood are attached. This base is covered over with a plaster made largely of mud; and a thatched roof, made of the leaves of palm trees, finishes the job. Some of the better houses, of course, are covered with tile. Until recently there was little electricity, and most of the people who wanted to keep in touch with the outside world did so with battery radios. By 1958, however, electricity was coming in to some of these places, bringing with it radios, motion-picture houses, and other evidences of our modern civilization. Roads, however, continue to be difficult—Jessie says they range from dusty to poor to non-existent. Usually our only means of transportation was by horse, mule, or on foot.

I recall once I was traveling through a district in southern Baía where large quantities of cacao—the chocolate bean—are grown. Several associates and I were on our way to hold a meeting in a church and were riding mules I had hired for the occasion. I was in front. As we reached the outskirts of the town of Itabuna, I noticed a young girl leaning out the window watching our group. I glanced up at her, and just at that moment my mule plunged into a mudhole. He began to jump and buck violently, and I was hurled off his back and into the mud. As I got out of the mudhole, thoroughly disgusted, and began to wipe some of the primordial ooze off my face and clothes, the girl at the window called down to me, in Portuguese, "Oh, mister, do that again. My mother didn't see it."

I remember another early experience when, traveling over the countryside in the hot sun, I became terribly thirsty. I had, of course, been warned not to drink anything but bottled water unless it had been boiled. But the man I was traveling with told me, "I can't stand it any longer. I'm going to have a drink of water." So we stopped at one of the thatched farmhouses. He talked to the farmer in Portuguese and I couldn't follow all that was said, but a moment later the farmer's wife came out with a tray of what looked like nice lemonade.

It looked so delicious, in fact, that I decided to have some myself. I took a big gulp. Lemonade, it certainly was not; water out of a mudhole, it almost certainly was. But mudhole or not, I drank it with the relish of a thirsty man. Fortunately, neither of us suffered any bad effects.

Wherever we went, we were treated as friends, and

there was always some home where we could spend the night. In most of these homes, however, we didn't sleep in beds but in hammocks we carried with us. Throughout northern Brazil, the individual hammock is part of one's personal equipment, as important as coat or hat or toothbrush is to us. Not only in the wilder interior but also in the cities, the homes have hammock hooks in almost every room, sometimes even in the kitchen. There are many advantages to this old custom. No matter how many people may drop in, there's always room to put them up for the night, for each will have his hammock with him and the host has only to help hang it on the hooks.

These hammocks are sometimes very elaborate. The hammock part itself is made of cotton. It may be hand-painted in lovely bright colors, or edged with fine lace that hangs down on the sides. In the interior sections, many of the people grow the cotton, spin the thread themselves, and have homemade looms where they weave their own "portable beds." Some of these homemade hammocks are truly works of art. I bought one with various scenes painted on the material with a homemade vegetable dye which, I was told, can never fade out.

The hammocks are about six feet long, with strings attached to each end to hang them up by. They are made in both double and single sizes—the former about fourteen feet wide, the latter about seven. They are hung up loosely, not stretched taut, and in some of the better houses the hooks are covered over with decorative plaster boxes set in the walls.

It is something of a trick to learn to sleep in a hammock; you have to sleep cater-cornered so that you can lie straight and turn as you please without any difficulty.

It was one of the most fascinating times of my life, those early years in Baía. The country was new and strange; so was the way of life of its people. At that time, Jessie usually stayed in the city to take care of the children, and I traveled widely throughout the state with one or two assistants. We would come into a community, the people would welcome us and invite us to dine. Sometimes we would have beans and rice and sweet potatoes—the latter fried, boiled and sliced, or candied. We might also have a coarse cabbage called *couve,* which is usually boiled. Dessert was often fried bananas, and when they were the plantains, which I consider the most delicious of all the varieties of bananas found in Brazil, I always took a second helping.

After sunset, around seven-thirty, we would usually hold our meeting. It might last an hour or an hour and a half, and much of it would be a song service. The Brazilians love to sing and many of them have truly fine voices. Then there would be a short message, perhaps, and prayers. After the meeting, we would go to the home where we were spending the night—it was often the house where the meeting was held—and we would sit around and talk; a few of these people always wanted to hear something about the city and what was going on that was new and exciting. The world loves to gossip a little, even in the backwoods of Baía. Around ten o'clock we would go to sleep in our hammocks. In the morning, as soon as it began to get light, life would begin anew.

Most of the people in these areas are farmers, but there are some who are called truckers. They are not really truckers in our sense of the word, they operate mule trains. Some of these men have as many as twenty or thirty mules and they contract with the individual farmers to carry their material down to the city. These mule trains are particularly useful in the southwestern area, where the terrain is more mountainous and the big oxcarts are too heavy to be hauled up the steep grades.

The mule train is like a caravan, with its eighteen or twenty loaded mules, a helper who runs alongside the animals to goad them on, and the muleteer who shouts and cracks his whip as they carry their loads into town.

Most of our first years in Baía, Jessie worked with other women in the community helping to build up our congregations. We had two churches in Baía when we left, both going strong. Jessie also continued to do her midwifery work, but she decided, finally, that this was not worth the tremendous effort involved, that her time and energy might better be spent in other ways.

As the children grew older and we found good people to look after them, Jessie became a little freer. Eventually she decided to take a trip into the interior with another lady of our church, on a selling tour of Adventist books and magazines. Perhaps she envied me my adventures.

In those days, ladies didn't travel alone and this tour of theirs was nothing short of revolutionary in that part of the world. Everywhere they went they were asked hundreds of questions. When Jessie would tell them she was married to an Adventist minister and missionary, they would look at her with redoubled interest.

This unique book-selling junket was all Jessie's idea and perhaps it would be well to let her report it in her own words—from the notes she wrote down sometime after she had returned to Salvador:

"Everybody was very surprised to see us because ladies

in those days weren't supposed to travel alone. We had a lot of big medical books with us and we knew the stores could sell these because they told people how to keep well —anything about health down there is always welcome.

"We hired a native to carry the books for us—at least a sample of them—in a high pile on top of his head. He would walk in front of us with the books on his head, and the people would stare at him and then at us and they would say, 'What have you there?' We would tell them these were medical books and we would always sell some.

"In one house where we stayed for some time—we always stopped with members of our church—I told the lady that I wasn't used to sleeping in hammocks. She said it was all right, I could sleep on a table. She put on a tablecloth first and that did make it a little softer but not much. We would roll up Turkish towels and put them under our hips and then it was not too bad.

"Wherever we went, people would ask us all kinds of questions about ourselves. When I told them I was married, they wanted to know how many children my husband and I had and they never could understand how we had only two children because in Brazil everyone has a big family.

"But they were always interested and kind to us, treated us well and bought books like hot cakes. I just couldn't seem to get enough. . . .

"On our first trip we spent ten days in the hinterlands of Baía, and there was never any trouble except with one poor man who couldn't seem to understand what we were doing. I was keeping my books stacked up in a store in a village and every time I'd stop in to pick some up he would come after me and put his face close to mine. Finally, I looked at him and said, 'Did you know the Lord is coming soon? It's just marvelous what the Bible tells us, isn't it?'

"He gave me a scared look and went out of the store. I never saw that tall man again, but many years later my husband went to that same town and stopped at that store. There was a tall man there and when he learned that my husband was an Adventist he told Leo, 'A long time ago there were two Adventist ladies here, and one of them was an angel.'"

Baía became our world and our home, and as we cooked and ate the native dishes and spoke the language, we became as much a part of this world as we had once been part of the Nebraska prairies.

Within a year after our arrival both Jessie and I spoke the language fairly well. I gave my first sermon in Portuguese in Baía after about fourteen months in Brazil. Following that came hundreds of more sermons in this language. Eventually it became as natural for us to talk in one tongue as in the other.

After the first sermon in Portuguese, however, I did not ask how many understood. I had heard about another American who gave his first sermon in Portuguese and ended by saying, "I want to know how many understood me. Will all those who understood what I have been saying please raise their hands."

In the grim silence that followed, not a single hand was lifted.

I avoided this possibility by just not asking.

I was still a lay minister in our church when I went to Brazil and for several years thereafter. It was in 1924 that I received a message from our church's South American headquarters in Buenos Aires—when Perón came to power it was transferred to Montevideo, Paraguay—summoning me to São Paulo. There was to be a board meeting, the message said, at which my family and I were expected.

I was glad for the chance to take Jessie, for she had not been well since Marian's birth and, although she was naturally a sturdy Nebraska farm girl, she had lost weight until she was down to a hundred pounds. A change of climate and environment, I thought, would do her a world of good.

We decided to make it a kind of vacation, so we went down to Rio and spent a couple of weeks there, enjoying the city's gaiety and color and cosmopolitan flavor. Then we went on to São Paulo.

São Paulo is known as the fastest growing city in the world. At the time of our first visit there, it had about half a million population; by 1958 it had grown to three million, and the figure appears destined to soar. Some people call São Paulo the Chicago of South America. The city is in the center of the coffee-growing area and once its entire wealth came from coffee. Now other industries have come in, and with them have come the airlines, so that São Paulo is now a center of air traffic. It is located on a high plateau, about 2,700 feet high, and the climate is generally mild and pleasant. It is today an ultra-modern city of wide streets and magnificent modern architecture. The population is as mixed as that of any North American city.

There are many Italians and Germans and recently, since the war particularly, Japanese. But no matter what their birth or descent, there is a great pride among them. The Paulistas, as they like to describe themselves, are somewhat like the Texans; everything must be the best and the biggest, whether it is the tropic vegetation, the palm-lined streets, the new gleaming pink-and-white buildings, the charm of the villages, or the vast reaches of the state of São Paulo itself, with its great coffee plantations rolling out as endlessly as the Texas plains.

This was the city to which we came on order of Division Headquarters. I had a notion that perhaps we would be given new orders or programs to carry out. To my surprise I found myself in the presence, not only of church directors of our South American division, but also of many ministers and lay members of the church.

I had been summoned for an ordainment ceremony, it turned out, and in the presence of this group, in a simple but moving ceremony, here in São Paulo, Brazil, I was ordained into the Gospel ministry.

We returned to Baía to throw ourselves back into the duties of our mission, which had grown by then into a complex organization, with two churches in the city itself and many smaller groups throughout Baía and several neighboring states. We were known by that time, and our work was known. In the city of Baía we had many friends among all groups, and many of them, even those not of our faith, gave us financial help. Thus we were able to aid more needy families in some of the poorer sections, and to carry on the other work of our mission.

But our eyes still looked to the north, toward our ultimate goal—the Amazon.

In 1927, our mission sent its first emissaries to the river— Elder John Brown and his wife. Elder Brown made a number of important contacts on his several trips to the interior. But because he had to depend on river boats to get from place to place, there were many areas he could not reach. The going was rough, even so, and within a few months he was stricken with a terrible tropical sickness and had to return to the United States to recuperate.

In 1928, three of our top division officers made a courageous and grueling trip to the headwaters of the Amazon and back, traveling through difficult country by boat and by muleback. On their return they agreed that our church must begin at once extensive missionary activity throughout the river world.

In November of that year, I received word from our division directors in Buenos Aires: Jessie and I were to prepare at once for a new assignment. It would involve drastic changes. We would have to prepare for an entirely new kind of life, get rid of most of our furniture, and tear up the roots we had sunk deep into the soil and soul of the Baía Mission and its people.

But what lay ahead for us was new and different and challenging, the letter said. We were to go to Belém, the city that lies at the mouth of the Amazon, and I was to begin work as director of a new mission that reached across the jungles and across the continent of South America to the Andes themselves.

This was our new assignment, mine and Jessie's—the vast sprawling outreach of the Amazon.

CHAPTER 5

DOORSTEP TO NOWHERE

THE Amazon is not a river but a vast mediterranean sea, a giant inland network of waterways, spread across the South American continent. At its mouth, which is more than two hundred miles wide, is the island of Marajó, as big as England. Close to three thousand miles in length, the river's hundreds of tributaries reach to within less than a hundred miles of the Pacific Ocean in Peru, and it extends its fingers into five other South American countries. Its deep, strong tributaries are navigable by big liners over more than fifty thousand miles of waterways. When the giant river floods, it inundates tens of thousands of square miles of land, often sweeping away farms and homesteads and entire villages.

We came to know this river world intimately over many years, Jessie and I. To know it and love it in many ways, and yet to be on guard against its hazards and its clutching, sometimes strangling, hands. If we can say that the Amazon is not a river but a sea, we can add that the country through which it flows is not a river valley but a world apart—partially known, largely unknown. It is a world of contrasts, of wilderness and riches, of emeralds and diamonds and mango fruit. It is a world of beauty and lush abundance, where everything seems able to grow in such profusion that a myriad of varieties of trees and flowers and herbs remain unclassified to this day. It is a world of splendor and savagery and of death along the riverbanks.

The powerful current of the Amazon spills out hundreds of millions of gallons of water into the Atlantic each second, and the water around its mouth is fresh for some three hundred miles out into the ocean. There is a famous story about a sailing ship some two hundred miles out from the mouth of the river that sent a signal to a passing steamer: "We are out of fresh water. Can you spare us some?"

Back came the reply from the liner: "Dip your buckets and drink."

The Amazon embraces with its color and romance and stifling heat and humidity an area almost as large as the entire United States. Much of it is colorful and romantic; much of it is unknown. The Green Hell of legend is not just one thing or place but many. There are places within this hell that are lovely as heaven on earth; and there are places where no man goes, where the intertwining vines and trees and undergrowth defy man to intrude. There are vast inundated regions, desolate and silent—drowned worlds. There are villages that stand mute and lonely against the jungle and the sky as the water recedes. it is a world that changes from one second to the next; a place of dread and violence one instant, a paradise of bright plumage and many-colored flowers the next.

To Jessie and me, it was—above all else—the people, the strange community of souls, half forgotten, half lost, almost swallowed up in the shifting lights and shadows of a tropic wilderness. They were a people who needed help in a hundred ways: people starving in the midst of plenty;

ravaged by disease in the midst of this humid lushness; people who hungered not for food so much as for a vision, for a reason to live, for purpose and goal and direction.

It was morning when we got our first look at the Amazon. We were still out of sight of land, but we could tell that we were entering the river mouth by the change in the color of the water. From the deep blue of the Atlantic, it had shifted to the yellow-orange we were to come to know so well.

There are, of course, many legends about this river. Its early history is wrapped in mystery and folklore and some fact. Much of it centers around a Spaniard named Francisco de Orellana, an explorer who was with Pizarro in Peru and left the main group to search for food. Following the river, he had a number of fantastic experiences, which included encounters with the "warrior women" who were said to be living along the river and who reportedly fought like men in battle. The women, so the stories go, were white and tall, and strong enough to shoot arrows that could pierce the planking of a brigantine. How much truth there was in all the many legends of these women is a matter of conjecture; the Spaniards, in any case, named the river after the lady warriors of Greek mythology because of these reports from Francisco de Orellana and his men.

I like best, perhaps, a legend told to us by an old Indian chief, as he looked at the river through his narrow, squinting eyes and spoke in his halting Portuguese:

"One evening just at the time of sunset," he told us, "the moon and the sun were in the sky at the same time, long ago, and the moon fell in love with the sun and its brightness and power and splendor, but the sun disdained the

moon and vanished over the edge of the earth and the
moon was left alone in the night and she fell to weeping
about all this, and her tears came down endlessly, it
seemed, and the tide of her tears spread out across the
whole continent, and so the river was born."

As the ship started upriver that first day, we stood on
deck, Jessie and I and our children—Jack was twelve then
and Marian eight—and it was there we got our first glimpse
of the jungle. That particular region was fairly well populated with small villages, and quite civilized. Yet it seemed
to us wild and dense. Just beyond the clearings, with their
handful of houses, along the banks, was a dark wall of foliage and brush and vines, twisted and contorted like some
senseless primitive painting. Green and orange and purple
and violet flowers mingled with the vines, which wrapped
parasitical fingers around the skyscraper trees, turning the
region into a mass through which, as we were to learn, one
had to cut his way with knife and machete.

Our destination lay just ahead. Belém—pronounced "Be-
leng"—is the capital city of the state of Pará and, like other
Brazilian state capitals, is sometimes called by the state
name. No one, of course, calls it by its full title—Nossa
Senhora de Belém de Grão Pará—which, literally translated, means Our Lady of Bethlehem of the Great River.

Belém is a truly tropical city, scarcely two degrees—120
miles—south of the equator. Unlike Baía, it is flat; but like
the city we had grown to think of as home, it is also a blend
of the old and the new. The handsome architecture of the
original Portuguese settlers slides away into narrow, dark
streets; along the docks crowd the humble homes of the
working people. There is a fantastic market place, officially

called the Docas de Vero Pêso, "the docks for looking up the weights."

Neither of us, of course, could guess how much Belém was to mean to us. It was to be our headquarters for nearly a quarter of a century, our only base apart from our boat, the *Luzeiro* itself. In many ways it was to become a central point in our lives and activities. But then it was only a new outpost to which we were coming to establish new churches and to begin our work in a "parish" that extended across the entire continent of South America. The total working staff of that "parish" was waiting for us on the dock. It consisted of three people. Two of them were what we call our colporteurs, or book salesmen. The third was the wife of one of them.

They had prepared for our coming by renting a two-story building, the second floor of which was to be our apartment. Downstairs was a big hall fitted out to be used as a church. This was to be called the Central Adventist Church of Belém.

They helped us get our things off the boat and hoisted up our trunks and valises and some of the packing cases of furniture to our new quarters. Within a few hours, Jessie had begun to transform the rooms into a real home.

Belém today is a city of perhaps 250,000 people. The old section is the most picturesque, with its narrow, twisting streets, its red-tiled roofs, its ancient buildings with gleaming blue-tiled fronts. Just as they had done in their native Portugal, the early settlers faced the entire fronts of their buildings with tile, which could easily be washed and never needed painting. Windows were open all day long and closed at night with shutters. In most of the homes there is no glass. A good-sized city with a good electric system, waterworks, streetcars, and a modern twentieth-century air, it is still an ancient Portuguese port town, and the smell of the sea and the Amazon is at its doorstep.

You get used to this strange mixture of the old and the new, the normal and the unusual. Once, years ago, the city fathers decided to install a new water system. They built a series of high tanks to hold the water—they are still visible for miles as you near the city—but when they turned on the water, the pressure from the high tanks broke every water main in town. These were gradually repaired, but the tanks remain as a crumbling memorial to that colossal engineering fiasco. All the time we lived in Belém, we found it necessary to boil our water, because of seepage in the city water pipes. (A new water system has been started as this is written.)

We arrived in the middle of the Brazilian rainy season—January, 1929. At that time of year the city is sodden and humid and far from exhilarating. But it was at least cheap. The apartment and the church hall below rented for 120 cruzeiros a month, at that time the equivalent of $12.

One of the first things we had to get used to was seeing people carry their burdens on their heads. The practice was—and still is—almost universal. We saw coffins, which are simple and unpainted as a rule, carried across town on the heads of the deceased's family. We watched in astonishment as five or six men hoisted a piano on their heads and calmly walked away with it. In the market, we became accustomed to calling a man to follow us around with a large tray on his head. We—like the local people—placed everything we bought on this large wooden tray. To fill up one of those trays with every kind of food in the market cost about the equivalent of a dollar.

In those first days there was no refrigeration, and meat had to be sold the day it was killed. Thus it was cheap in the morning; would go up in price around noon as the supply became scarce; and as the hours went on, the price would drop again on whatever was left. Sometimes the markets would display live alligators, jaws tied, and customers who were hungry for this "delicacy" would come along and chop off pieces of the meat from the live animal, beginning at the tail.

In the big public market we could buy the rarest fruits on earth, hundreds of varieties out of the jungle. There were all kinds of bananas and nuts and beans, papayas and cassavas and lemons. But many of the foods we were used to were rare and expensive; potatoes, which had to be imported, were beyond our means. Milk was available usually only in powdered form, and we almost never saw carrots.

The city itself was and is a blend of the two worlds that meet here, the civilized modern world with all the latest improvements and the tropical jungle world that holds Belém in a green embrace. Sometimes the two meet under odd circumstances.

When a visitor from the United States asked a lady who lived in Belém about the peril of snakes in the city, she replied with what she considered justifiable annoyance, "Snakes in Belém? Well, I've lived here fifteen years and never even saw one. Of course, you might try the zoo!"

As she was telling him this, they heard something pounding and scraping under the floor in her living room. When the noise continued, her husband called in a carpenter, who took up the boards of the floor. There, to the visitor's delight and the lady's embarrassment, lay a boa constrictor, living contentedly in a small space just under the player piano.

In another instance, a recently arrived Englishman set up his hammock on the front porch one Sunday morning and was settling down with the newspapers when he saw something coming down one of the posts. He called his assistant, who told him it was a baby boa. They got a basket and put the boa safely away in it. A few minutes later another of the same size slithered down. They captured it. Before the morning was gone they had caught forty-eight baby boas on the porch of their recently rented home.

When the Englishman, extremely upset, spoke to the landlord about this, the latter was effuse in his apologies. "I'd forgotten to tell you, it just slipped my mind," he explained to the startled Englishman. "A few years ago I put a pair of boas up in the attic to keep the rats and mice and such things away from the house. So—that's where the youngsters came from."

The Englishman and the landlord went at once to investigate the attic and found the two boas still there. The Englishman handed the basket of baby boas to the landlord. "If you don't get rid of these creatures and their parents, we are leaving."

We grew used to the bizarre and the sometimes tragic in Belém, where we were settling down to organize our church, to recruit members, and to build our organization. One instance that occurred some years after our arrival involved a young lady who played the organ for our services.

She was a very beautiful girl when she began to work with us, but after two years she began to change. Both

Jessie and I noticed it, and after Jessie examined her she was obliged to tell the mother that she thought the daughter had leprosy.

The mother was indignant and insisted it simply could not be true. In Belém at that time were Ferdinand Stahl and his wife—he was the author of the book on the Incas which had influenced us to come into the mission field. At Jessie's request, he and his wife looked at the girl. Both had seen many cases of the disease in their explorations and they confirmed Jessie's diagnosis. "She has leprosy," they told us. "You must separate her at once from the rest of the family and see that she uses separate dishes."

The mother agreed. She also promised to call health authorities to make an official examination of the girl. The authorities came and made a mucus test. For about three months there was no report on their findings. Then it came through: The authorities said their reports indicated she was perfectly well.

I still remember how the mother of this beautiful girl came to our apartment and shook the report in Jessie's face and cried out, "I knew my girl did not have leprosy."

"Oh, I wish I could rejoice with you," Jessie answered, "but I do not believe that report, and if you do nothing to arrest this case—then—"

She left her sentence unfinished and the woman stalked angrily out and down the stairs. But the girl's condition became worse, day by day, until the authorities who had pronounced her "perfectly well" would not allow her on the streets. Ultimately—too late for retardation of the illness to any degree—she was taken to the leper colony. As this is written, the terrible scourge has cost her ears and eyes.

Meantime, because no precautions had been taken, another girl in the family contracted the disease and was also sent to the leper colony.

Such incidents were rare in Belém. Not often were boas found in attics or lovely young girls sent off to leper colonies. Yet these things happened; they were part of the world in which we began to organize our church.

For these first months I stayed close to the city itself, studying conditions, learning as much as I could from the people who were already interested in our Adventist church, and making plans. One of my plans was an immediate down-to-earth one—for a calcium carbide projector which would enable me to show my slides. I took them to a local tinner who seemed fascinated with them and agreed to make the projector but wanted to know what it was being used for.

When I told him it was for a religious meeting, he asked me more questions. Could he come and bring his wife? He could, and he did. The tinsmith and his family were the first family to come into our Belém church. Soon, as word spread, there were more. Almost at once we started a Sabbath school for the children.

This organizing work in Belém might not have gone so swiftly had it not been for a kind of advance guard we'd had in the person of the colporteurs. Certainly no man could hope to grow rich in such work, particularly in a predominantly Catholic country where many people had no knowledge of any Protestant faith. Yet they gave their lives to carrying Bibles and books and pamphlets into obscure villages along the riverbanks and the narrow tributaries of the Amazon. Transportation was always difficult; they were limited to river steamers or travel by smaller boat; with no large funds available, they usually traveled by canoe.

One of these men was Andre Godrath, an Englishman who had come to Brazil half a century before and had dedicated his life to selling religious and health literature. His adventures in the sale of books are a story all by themselves. In 1930, just a year after our arrival in Belém, Dr. Getulio Vargas and his followers staged a revolution and overthrew the government, establishing Vargas as dictator over all Brazil. During this period there was great agitation to keep down communism, which had already begun infiltrating some areas of Brazil. The newly formed government was particularly vigilant against this peril, and police in local areas were alerted to be on guard against all persons who did not fit the accepted patterns of thought at that critical juncture.

Andre was at that time selling his books in a nearby community. For reasons beyond my understanding, one of his prospective customers apparently grew suspicious when Andre tried to sell him a volume entitled *Twelve Great Signs of Our Lord's Return,* and asked him to explain the book a little. When Andre got to the chapter which suggests that capital and labor should work together in harmony to carry out the commands of the Lord, a policeman stepped out from behind a tree and arrested him. Without formal trial, he was hurried off to jail and placed in solitary confinement. He had only a hard bench on which to sleep, no fresh air, and no sanitary facilities. The food was very coarse, and as he was already suffering from a stomach disorder he nearly died of starvation.

For eleven days this man suffered in that jail. There was no organization of ours in the town to come to his aid. A

Presbyterian minister who heard about his plight sent him a hammock to sleep on and milk and food each day.

On Christmas Eve came a kind of amnesty from the new government: all Brazilian prisoners accused of being communist agitators were to be freed, as a gesture of Christian forgiveness. But this gesture did not extend to accused foreigners—and Andre was English. Instead of releasing him, in fact, his jailer informed Andre that he was to be shot on New Year's Day.

During that week Andre spent most of his time in prayer. His attitude, as I found out later when I learned the story, was that he did not mind dying as a witness for Jesus but he did not want to die falsely accused of being a communist.

On the day that he was to be taken out and shot, he was led beforehand into court for what could have been a perfunctory trial and condemnation. But I believe that the Lord must have heard his prayer. As he came into the court, he miraculously met a lawyer whom he had known for some time and to whom he had sold some of his religious books. The lawyer was in court on other business but at once agreed to help Andre. With the lawyer's help, Andre was soon set free.

This wonderful man and his work were known in many of the villages and backwash settlements in the tidal basin around Belém, as well as in remote villages which it scarcely seemed possible for a man to reach, traveling alone in a twelve-foot canoe, loaded down with pamphlets and books.

I remember one place that I reached with several visiting church officials after a five-day steamer trip up the Amazon and a three-day trip on muleback over jungle trails into the interior. It was a village called Jeru, a one-

street town with houses built on both sides of a three-mile
stretch of road. As we rode on our mules, people peered
out of every doorway to see the strangers.

We had come to Jeru because we had heard that there
were many persons in the town who were interested in
our work. And as we rode down the "Main Street" of the
jungle, we came to a house with a sign on it reading:
"Seventh-day Adventist School." This, in a village where
the only Adventist visitor before us had been book salesman Andre Godrath.

The man who taught in this school took us to his home.
Unlike most of the other houses in this village, the teacher's
home was immaculate and well kept. The teacher obviously practiced what he taught.

As I glanced around the living room of this pleasant
home, I noticed a large frame on the wall. In it there were
several pictures. In the upper right-hand corner was a picture of the president of Brazil; in the lower corner was a
picture of one of the governors of the state; along the sides
were smaller photographs of other government officials.
But in the center of this frame, mounted on gold paper,
was a picture of Andre Godrath, the seller of religious
literature.

The teacher explained to us, "It was he who brought us
the books and told us about them and changed our lives."

These sellers of religious literature for our faith regard
themselves rightly as front-line workers. Their canoes, in
the Amazon and its tributaries, become their homes—their
bedrooms, kitchens, and dining rooms. In the front of the
canoe will be a "stove" made from a kerosene can and fire
clay on which they cook their food—beans usually, and
rice, with whatever vegetables they can obtain along the

way. The books are covered over with two thicknesses of palm leaves, with large banana leaves in between, to shed the rain.

Their experiences are often startling. It is not unusual for a fish to jump into the boat and save a weary salesman the trouble of foraging for his supper. Sometimes at night an alligator will attack the canoe and try to tip it over. To guard against this, our colporteurs are furnished with canoes that rise at least eighteen inches above the water— too high for an alligator to overturn.

Often at night a colporteur will paddle into a narrow channel where he can tie up to a tree and where the waves will not be high enough to be dangerous, as they would be on the wide river if a storm should strike. But this is no guarantee of safety—or of a night without excitement.

One night one of our colporteurs, a Brazilian named Pedro Bernardo, had tied up to a limb of a tree in one of these channels and gone to sleep in his canoe. It was dark when he tied up his boat, so he had not realized that the tree to which he tied was covered with thousands of what are called fire ants. These creatures get their name from the fact that their bite is terribly painful, like fire, and lasts a long time. Of course, an army of that size could have destroyed him.

Pedro, however, slept peacefully in his canoe, unaware of this invading force crawling silently through the dark over the line from the tree limb to the canoe.

While the colporteur slept on, a gust of wind stirred the canoe, turning it so that one side touched the limb of another tree on which were hundreds of black ants, slightly larger than the fire ants and their deadly enemies.

Down the limb into the canoe, silently in the dark of the

night, came the black ants to meet and do battle with the fire ants.

They met in the canoe, about a foot from the head of the sleeping seller of religious books. When Pedro awoke in the morning, he discovered their battlefield, strewn with piles of dead ants, while over the line from the canoe to the tree the black ants were still pursuing the fire ants and battling with them all the way to their nests.

Only then was Pedro aware of the protection he had received that night as he slept in the dark after his hard day's work.

We know of many other instances of the protection that seemed to hover over these men. One involved two colporteurs who were making their rounds together, carrying a heavy pack of books to show. At one house, as they set their pack down to open a fence gate, one of the young men stepped back into the tall grass momentarily, and a bushmaster, one of the deadliest snakes in the Amazon, bit him just above the ankle.

They had no anti-snakebite serum, and the only other treatment possible was the ancient native Indian technique —to light a fire and burn the bitten leg to a crisp to destroy the poison. The bitten man understandably did not relish the idea of the fire treatment.

"We are either doing the Lord's work or we are not," he told his associate. "If it is the Lord's work and He desires that I deliver these books to those who have ordered them, then I am going on and do that work right now. And if He does not intend that I should do so, then I am willing that His will be done."

The two men found a stick and killed the snake, and

then they knelt down in the path and prayed. After that they picked up their books and went on their way.

As they went on with their work, the man virtually forgot that he had been bitten by a deadly snake. The wound did not even swell, the bitten man told me later. In the gospel of St. Luke there is a verse: "I give unto you power to tread on serpents and nothing by any means shall hurt you."

To help Andre in his work in our newly opened-up Amazon mission district, we had a boat built for him—actually the first of our boats along the river. It was seventeen feet long and had only meager facilities for travel, but it marked the beginning of our expanded activity and it was designed to make Andre's life easier and his work more effective. After we built this craft, in 1930, two of our directors came to Belém from Rio de Janeiro and we arranged a trip—my first trip up the Amazon beyond Belém. Jessie did not go on this trip but stayed at home with the children.

We did not start in the little boat, which we called *The Messenger*, but carried the craft along with us on a long river steamer—a twin-ruddered vessel built to carry five hundred passengers. There were screened-in cabins for first-class passengers, a promenade deck, and a music hall. Third-class passengers traveled on the lower deck and swarmed in like flies, people of many types and racial mixtures. There were no sleeping quarters; everyone slept in his own hammock, which was attached to bulkheads or posts. At night it was impossible to walk through the lower deck, honeycombed as it was with hundreds of hammocks.

The steamer, like most of the others of its type on the Amazon, carried no refrigeration. Below decks were tethered about a dozen steers. Each day we would stop while some of the crew went out along the banks of the river and cut grass to feed the animals. And each day one or two of the steers would be butchered, so we always had fresh meat on board.

When we ran out of steers, the ship would stop at one of the farms along the river and the sailors would go out and lasso a wild bull. Everyone was out on deck to watch as the animal was forced into a canoe and brought out to the boat—usually with much difficulty and thrashing about —and ultimately hoisted on board, weighed, and put down in the hold. The following day it would be served for dinner.

After about seven days we arrived at the pleasant, tropical town of Parintins, and our boat was lowered over the side. Our pilot and guide, Andre, the two men from Rio, and I went ashore. The next day we planned to start up a small stream to a community where there were some Adventists who wanted to talk about forming a church.

We lazed through the tropical afternoon, talking of the journey to come; then to cool off we went for a swim in the crystal-clear waters of a little river, the Pirama de Limao. We were enjoying ourselves immensely in the cool water when suddenly a man came running out of the woods, calling to us, "Get out of the river—get out!"

We looked at him in surprise. "There are only two kinds of people who swim in this river," he shouted. "Drunkards and mad men."

I was about to ask him why, when I glanced behind me and saw in the water where we were swimming about a dozen alligators, any of which would have relished a leg or arm.

One part of this journey took us to Cinco Kilos,* an Indian village, far up the Maués River, about six hours above the town of Maués—distances on the river are measured almost exclusively in the hours or days it takes to go from one place to the next.

It was our plan to meet with the Indians, make friends with the chief, and perhaps pave the way for holding one or two meetings. One of the directors from Rio had brought along, as a good-will offering, a trunkload of tin whistles. These he handed out to every man, woman, and child in the tribe. This giveaway program was a magnificent triumph; from the first moment on, the din of the whistles nearly drove us mad. After some hours the chief himself couldn't take it any longer and sent out an order for quiet.

While his tribe sat around admiring the whistles they had been forbidden to blow, we talked with the old chief of some of the legends of the river and of Brazil, and he told us the story of the guarana, a flowering vine that bears fruit which at first looks something like ground cherries, but which later opens up to resemble the eye of a child.

Once, the old chief explained, there was a little girl who was very beautiful and who had magic power to heal. One day the witch doctor, according to the legend, became so jealous that he slipped up behind this fairy child and clubbed her to death. Then everyone was sad. But another fairy appeared and told the people to take the child's eyes and plant them, and so they did, and the plant still looks like a child's eyes and still has power to heal any illness.

There is a process of mashing the kernels of these berries

---

* Years before, the Indians of that village had collected a ball of rubber weighing five kilos and sold it for a large sum of money. To commemorate the event, the local chief renamed the village.

into a kind of dough, baking it until hard, and grating it by using the dried, hard, sandpaper tongue of a big Amazon fish called the pirarucú. The result is a product that has five times as much caffein as coffee. Taken this way it becomes a terrible habit and one very difficult to break. And who knows—maybe, as the old chief insisted, it cures something, if only drowsiness.

A diluted form of this product is now manufactured in vast quantities and sold as a soft drink throughout Brazil, where it has become extremely popular.

We talked with the chief of this and other matters of interest along the river, and after we had won his confidence he invited us to have dinner with him and to hold a religious meeting afterward.

The chief's house was a well-built structure, with beautiful ceilings of straw matting woven with great delicacy and art. Dinner was extraordinarily simple: the Indians lit a big fire and brought in a monkey they had killed. One fellow grabbed it by the tail and another by the front legs, and they pulled it back and forth over the open fire until all the hair was singed off. Then they cut it open, cut off the feet, and put it in a kerosene can to boil. As the water in the five-gallon can began to boil, a little paw kept appearing over the top of the can, for all the world as if it were saying good-by. Then it would disappear again.

Bananas in the tropics are a great blessing. They were all we could eat for dinner that night.

Sometime later, after this chief's conversion, one of his proud boasts was, "We don't eat monkey meat any more."

When it was time for the meeting—the first I had ever held among Indians—about fifty people crowded into a little room in the chief's house, and we began by trying to teach them to sing some hymns. One was "Jesus Loves Me, This I Know," which they liked so much they insisted on singing it over and over. Then our director from Rio gave the prayer while the Indians bowed their heads reverently.

After that I stood up to begin my sermon. Only four of the group understood Portuguese, so I had one of them translate for me. I started with John 3:16: "For God so loved the world, that he gave his only begotten Son, that whosoever believeth in him should not perish, but have everlasting life." Then I built around this verse, telling how Jesus had been born in a manger, how He grew up, and finally how He loved us so that He gave His life to redeem us from sin.

As I spoke, I noticed that my interpreter seemed to be saying the same words over and over. I called one of the others to my side and asked if the interpreter was actually getting across what I was trying to tell them. The man explained that my interpreter didn't want to take upon himself the responsibility for what I was saying, so he prefaced each and every sentence with, "The white man says. . . ."

After that, I went on speaking, and despite this difficulty I could see tears in the eyes of some of these men and women, as I talked. When I asked how many wanted to know more about the life of our Lord, every hand went up instantly.

These Maués River Indians had, of course, had previous contact with traders, and so were not frightened by white men and had no inclination to run from their villages when we appeared. Yet they were primitive in many ways and wore practically no clothes at all. Indeed, in the midst of the service, a young girl about sixteen years old came down the center aisle of the room, stark naked. No one appeared concerned in the least except the old chief, who stood up and spoke a few words to her quietly. She left and came back in a moment, wearing a shawl.

This was the way these people lived at the time we first went there. We eventually started a group among them, and built a schoolhouse there.

We went on down the Maués River after the meeting, back to the city of Maués. Near there was the man who had sent us up to preach to the Indians and we stopped for a brief visit with him. His name was Jose Baptista Michiles, and he was the first Brazilian in the Amazon district to come into our church; one of the colporteurs had brought him some literature, which had changed his life.

Michiles was a man of some means and vast influence throughout the valley. He had large land holdings with more than nine hundred head of cattle and grew other crops, including Brazil nuts. He had many people working for him, and a number of them came into our church as a result of his example. The Michiles family came to be our good friends. His wife was part Indian and they had six children—all were sent to our college in São Paulo and all are now college graduates.

When we reached Maués on this return trip, I was anxious to send a message to Jessie in Belém, since she had had no word from me for some days. The man in the telegraph office, however, explained that the machine had broken down and no one in the city knew how to fix it. I got out the kit of tools I had taken with me, and after three hours I had the machine operating and was able to send my message.

We went on up the river to Manaus and then on back

down the river in our little boat. There we ran into trouble. We came to one point where we could save about five hours if we could take a short cut by way of a narrow stream. We asked one of the natives if the water was deep enough for our boat, and he assured us it was three feet or more—ample for our craft. So we started down this narrow stream. It was about five or six feet wide with high grass growing on both sides, and the sensation was something like riding in a ditch through endless hayfields.

But it did not go on very far for us. Suddenly we found ourselves aground in less than ten inches of water. Because the current was strong even if the water was shallow, it was impossible for us to back up or to try to push the boat against that current. We decided that our best move would be to go ahead, even if it meant that we had to drag the boat over the mud.

Since this was Andre's boat, to be used in delivering his books, we had accepted him as the captain, and in this crisis he proved his stamina. Our only chance was for all of us to get out of the boat and push, Andre stated firmly. There was danger in the mud and the tall grass—snakes and other creatures that could bring destruction. "And anybody who doesn't get out, I'll throw out," the old man added for extra emphasis.

We did as the gnarled veteran of the Amazon Valley ordered. We sank into mud and slime that held peril at every step, and together we strained and pushed and hauled the boat across the shallow areas. It was a grueling, sweating, hazardous business but somehow we kept at it, goaded and coaxed and badgered by that white-haired man who would not give up.

It was not too long before the water began to deepen,

and after close to an hour of pushing we found ourselves over the shallow part and back again into deep water. We ran into one terrible storm on the rest of our trip down the Amazon but managed to get into one of the little side streams to ride it out.

When we reached Belém, I learned that Jessie and the children, far from leading sedate and uneventful lives, had been in the center of a minor revolution, most of which had been fought out with wild gunplay directly in front of our house.

Across from our house was a newspaper office, the largest building in town. The paper was opposed to the policies of the government and was not afraid to say so editorially. Apparently the government officials suspected, or said they suspected, that the building was to be used as the center of a revolt. Soldiers were sent to put down the rebellion—and, if possible, to force the paper out of business.

Jessie and the youngsters, of course, had no idea of all this. They had been asleep when shots began to ring out. Our police dog, whose job it was to protect them, had crawled under the bed in fright.

The children and our maid and Jessie got down on their knees and prayed. "You don't need to be afraid," Jessie told them. "We will be protected."

The fighting continued sporadically through the night. One man, Jessie told me, was shot right on our front steps, and in the morning the maid had to go down and wash off the blood.

The next day men arrived with crowbars, determined to smash their way into the office of the newspaper. But the owner had outguessed them. He had obtained a high-tension transformer to step up the voltage and electrify the front door. When the men tried to break in with crowbars, three of them fell dead.

The result was a kind of stalemate, but the owner had saved his paper from the invaders. Brazilians have a stubborn streak of independence, something like that of early New England.

Right or wrong, they stick by their beliefs even unto death.

But now it was almost time for our furlough back to the States. We had delayed it for a year in order to go to the Amazon and to learn about conditions there so we would know what was most needed to serve these people.

I knew the answer now, after this trip.

"We cannot do our full job or even a major part of it here in Belém, or by taking trips up the river on the steamers," I told Jessie. "We're going to have to have our own boat so that we can go wherever we have to go."

We talked a long time about this. I would have to design a boat myself, we decided, and build it here in Belém, after our return from the States. I knew nothing about building boats and not very much about navigation, and the Amazon is a wide and treacherous river and a challenge even to the most experienced sailors.

But such considerations, Jessie and I agreed, were merely details beside the far greater challenge of bringing help to the people of the river.

CHAPTER 6

LOGBOOK

"APRIL 10. Pulled anchor at 3:10. Nice morning. Little moon and two beautiful stars in east. At 6:20 the motor began to heat so the boy got in and found grass in propeller. Motor cooled down to normal. . . .

"April 13. During the night a big island came floating down the small river and caught our boat, broke the big limb of the tree that we tied to, and pressed us into the trees along the bank and broke one window glass. . . .

"April 15. Quiet night. Lots of rain. Left at 5 and at 11 we saw a big bunch of orchids in a tree, so stopped and got the bunch, twenty-five flowers on one plant. Passed mouth of Rio Branco and at 7 stopped in front of a small town called Carveeira for night."

So read a few scattered excerpts of the day-to-day notes I kept in pen or pencil in a five-cent copybook—the log of the *Luzeiro.*

In the woods of the Amazon, a monster of a tree spills over with a giant roaring protest as it crashes down into the undergrowth. It has been centuries in the growing, but now it is to be snaked out of the woods, floated down the stream, and brought finally to the boat yard in Belém where the boat I've designed is to be built. So we began to make our craft out of the sinews of the jungle world it was to serve.

But to reach that point there had been a long time of preparation. Our furlough was not merely a time for rest and visiting and gathering around the family table back in Nebraska to relate all our exciting adventures. It was a time for making a tour of many states. Throughout America, particularly along the West Coast, we talked to both children and adults about our work and plans.

Our Missionary Volunteer Societies helped, and the children's groups worked hard to raise contributions. When we returned to Belém in 1931, after our year's leave, we had collected enough to build our boat—$5,400.

Meanwhile, I had been giving myself a full-fledged course in boatbuilding. I read and studied everything I could find on the subject. I studied problems of navigation such as we expected to encounter on the Amazon with its currents, its tributaries, the floating islands of grass, the flooded areas and tidal lakes.

On the ship taking us back to Belém, I got out my drafting materials and began to design our craft. I had learned quite a lot about small boats. I also had to figure on the special problems of the Amazon: the need for a sturdy craft because of the storms which are often accompanied by high waves, yet the need as well for a shallow-draft boat because of wide variations in tides and depths, and the difficulty of getting into some of the little ports along the rivers when the water is low.

The boat I designed was thirty-three feet long, ten feet wide, and drew only two and a half feet of water. It had a double-V bottom—the two V's ran the length of the boat, one on each side, with a space between. The bottom was designed in a convex curve slightly higher at the center keel than at the edges. This gave us a little dead space under the boat that helped to keep the boat steady. The double V was useful in many ways. The boat would stand safely on its V-shaped haunches when the tide ran out, and this gave us an easy method of cleaning the bottom or making emergency repairs on a mud flat miles from civilization.

Once the boat was on paper, I had to have materials and a place to build. I found a yard in Belém—where, in fact, we had built *The Messenger* for Andre—but the man who owned it was dismayed at my design, told me it was unlike anything he had ever heard of, and said it would turn over the moment it hit the water. He finally agreed to let me build it in his yard but only on condition that I would not hold him responsible for the disaster he was certain would come with the launching.

I hired a man who knew Brazilian woods to get my lumber, and we sat down and figured out what we would need. The keel was to be made of an ironlike wood called *pau de arco*. The main planking was to be of *itatuba*, one of the toughest woods known to man. Twelve trees were needed for the planking, and eight of the larger trees to make the ribs. Six large cedars went into the finishing woodwork for the boat. All of these had to be brought out of the jungle, down to Belém. It took two months.

The planks that went into the *Luzeiro* were one and a fourth inches thick, eight inches wide, and thirty-three feet long. The trees out of which they were hewn were several hundred years old at least, for they grow slowly. There is no way of knowing their exact age. There are no age circles on trees in the tropics because there are no wide variations in the seasons or the rate of growth. In the Amazon jungle, the variety of hardwood trees alone is said to number more than 450.

Cut in the jungle about fifty-five miles west of Belém, on the Muju River, these trees were dragged out by oxen to a small stream, floated to a larger stream and then on down to Belém. This was harder than it sounds, for itatuba logs will not float and we had to fasten lighter-weight trees to these logs to get them downstream. Naturally, when they are shaped into planks and put into place on a boat, they float. The itatuba has a kind of emery in its veins, a grit it seems to draw up from its roots. Because of this, it burns up the teeth of a power saw. There are only two ways to cut this wood. One is to use a hand saw, sawing up and down through the log lengthwise, with a high sawhorse, and one man sawing from a level above the other.

The other is to square the log up with a broad ax and then cut little notches at just the width desired for a board. Sawdust and kerosene are put in these grooves and a match touched to them. This cracks the wood in a straight line at the desired point. After the same thing is done on the other end of the log, wedges are driven into the grooves and the rough board is split off and trued up to exact measurement with an ax. It is a hard job and most of our planks were sawed off with the hand saw, which wasn't quite so difficult.

The ribs we made of piquia, a wood with a grain that is twisted and curled; it can be cut into odd shapes without splitting. I drew out the patterns myself on thin pieces of wood, and from these the actual ribs were made with a hand saw and a narrow blade. Then we set the work to lay the keel.

It was a primitive boat yard, with no circular saws, no power saws, no planing machines. At that time virtually everything had to be done by hand. I was in the boat yard most of the time, while Jessie carried on much of the daily work of our church. Jack would bring over lunch for me at noon and I would work right through the heat of the day.

The boat-yard operator, Alfonso Mallo, still insisted our craft wouldn't float. But he did watch our progress with increasing interest, and asked many questions. I explained some of my innovations. He went over my plans again and finally agreed that perhaps he had been hasty. He had never before seen a craft like ours, but there *was* a chance it might stay right side up.

By the time our hull was finished, our motor had arrived—a two-cylinder, twenty-horsepower diesel I had bought for approximately $700 from a Belém dealer. I had put in the wiring myself. Now we were able to put in the motor, hook up the propeller and the electric equipment. By the remote-control system I had developed, the motor could be started like a truck from the driver's seat.

Of course, we had brought back with us from the States many things hard to find in Brazil: winch, anchor, anchor chain, an auxiliary motor for an electric-light plant, little stoves for cooking. Our china and silver and stainless steelware were from home. Most of our other equipment —bedding, mattresses, sheets, and towels—we bought in Brazil. Our stoves were of the kind called primeless pressure cookers and worked with kerosene. They were good and provided a kind of elemental pressure-cooking system, but they made a terrible noise that frightened Jessie out of the kitchen the first time we tried them.

At last she was finished. She was a strange-looking craft, I had to admit, more like a houseboat than a river-going launch. Yet she was sleek and slim, bright and sparkling, with her white paint and gray-and-black trim. I was as proud and excited as I had been as a youth, with my first long pants.

July 4, 1931—approximately three months after we had begun to search for wood—the *Luzeiro* was launched. Jessie christened her with a bottle of imitation champagne that was simply soda water while forty of our church people watched. The *Luzeiro* slid down the ways and floated nicely—exactly at the line I had marked as the center of buoyancy.

The first man on board was the boat-yard owner, effusive with his excited congratulations.

We spent a couple of hours making a trial run around Belém harbor. All was well. We brought the boat back to finish the painting and to take on our final stores—beans, rice, sugar, sacks of flour, matches, and our medical supplies, of course. On this first trip they were limited—basically they consisted of quinine, medicine for hookworm, Epsom salts, castor oil, and headache pills.

We spent all afternoon loading the boat, had our evening meal at home, and then went back on board. About eleven o'clock the tide was in and we moved to deep water in the harbor and anchored for our first night on board. We had with us our children, Jack and Marian, and our good friend, Andre.

Of course, we had to spend a while looking everything over, like children examining toys at Christmas. We looked not once but several times, and we didn't miss a single detail.

The boat was divided into four basic parts: Forward was a large room that served as a combination living room, dining room, bedroom, and navigating room. There were three beds that were hung on the wall by leather straps and came down at night like Pullman berths. Two hung lengthwise by the windows, one crosswise in front. All were completely curtained for privacy. There were two additional sofas under the window beds, so we could sleep five comfortably if necessary.

Behind this main room was the engine room. Then came the bath and sanitary installations; and in the stern was the galley. Everything was snug and shipshape with storage of oil tanks below decks and other supplies in cabinets and drawers. We hadn't wasted one cubic inch of space.

I can honestly say that this was one of the happiest nights of my life. After we had finished our inspection and climbed into our berths, I lay there trying to grasp the reality: We had reached a milestone in our work. We were here, we knew the language, and we had our own boat. With it we could go to the most remote places of the Amazon, where lived people we had never before been able to reach.

We were up early to catch the tide, and were under way before dawn. We were heading upstream, almost due west, toward a sixty-mile-wide bay called the Baía de Marajó, formed where the Tocantins River spills into the Amazon. The day dawned clear and cloudless. The tide was behind us and the wind, of course, came in from the sea—the trade winds always blow from east to west on the Amazon. Because we were going with the tide and the current, there were no waves.

Jessie cooked breakfast. It was a kind of celebration that morning; we had fried eggs and toast and chocolate.

The day was full of excitement—and satisfaction. The *Luzeiro* behaved perfectly, and I found that my do-it-yourself course in navigation had paid off. While Jack and Marian ran from one end of the boat to the other, and Jessie became acquainted with her kitchen, we crossed the dangerous sixty-mile stretch that was the bay and kept on up the south bank of the river into what is called the Straits of Brevis or the Narrows, a strange, spider-web world of hundreds of little rivers that flow through and around and past these islands.

We anchored long after dark that night in a narrow stream, somewhat offshore.

And then we began to learn the fantastic sounds of the woods and the river: the giant bullfrogs, the big rats of the woods called *toros,* the alligators, the insects. Later we were to grow used to them, but that first night they were all new and strange.

Oddest of all were the howling monkeys, which live all along the river. These are small, reddish-brown animals who seem to delight in putting on symphony concerts about four o'clock in the morning. They even have a musical director who gives a recognizable signal that starts them off. Once this sounds, the woods come alive with hideous noises—something like a bunch of hogs grunting. The symphony starts off softly, and the noise gradually builds up into a grand crescendo. Then, on another signal from the musical-director monkey, it stops. All is silent. The quiet is impressive and lasts for about a minute. Then the next number begins.

All these monkeys are huddled together in a group in the woods, and when they begin their concert they shake the limbs of the trees in rhythm. After one group has performed for ten minutes or so, it will halt and another orchestra, closer or farther away, will take up the performance.

As the days passed and we drew farther and farther away from civilization, we saw nature as we had never known it existed. Leaping fish and birds of every type and color; great flocks of white herons—so many hundreds of them that their wings seemed like white clouds. And odors! In the early morning, particularly, the smell of the woods is like perfume and flowers and earth, melons and rain and giant dripping leaves, all blended together.

We had been heading up streams on our way west, often getting into *paranás*, as the small rivers are called, getting lost, and having to find our way back to the main stream. Sometimes Andre himself had no idea of our whereabouts. On our first Sabbath we anchored along the way for morning service and weekly Sabbath school. We were sitting there studying our Bibles and singing a few hymns together when I looked out over the bright-yellowish water and saw, coming toward us, an old man in a canoe. He came up to our boat, excused himself for interrupting our religious service, and asked a question I have since heard many thousands of times on the river, "Mister, have you any medicine for the fever?"

"Yes, we have some medicine," I answered. "Who is sick?"

"In my home a number of people are sick. All of my family are there and they are all sick with the fever." Then he added, "We live up the river from here. Will you come to help us?"

I assured him that we would but that it would take us a little time to get under way again.

"How will you know which house it is?" he asked.

"That's simple," I said. "When you hear our boat, come outside your house and wave a white towel."

When we reached that spot on the river a short time later, however, he wasn't in front of the house. He was sitting in his canoe in the middle of the stream waving a big white sheet.

I will never forget the sight that greeted us as we went into his house. The roof and walls were of thatched palm leaves, held up by poles on the sides and with one main support in the middle of the one large room. From that center post, radiating out to the side walls like spokes of some giant, quivering wheel, were twenty-one hammocks, and in each of these was someone who was sick.

Some were shaking with the malaria chills. Others were burning with high fever, motionless and gaunt. Still others had broken out into a cold sweat. At that time all we had with us to treat this disease was quinine; more specific drugs and treatments were to come years later. But quinine we had. We sterilized our needles and began to inject it. It was obvious that the treatment did good, not only medically but psychologically; someone was doing something, these people were not merely being left there to die.

When we had finished with the injections, the old man said to me, "Mister, would you please sing some of these

hymns that I heard you singing when I was coming to your
boat?"

So we opened our book and sang to them; and I read
from the Bible, and prayed, asking the Lord to heal them.

The man asked us to go to other houses in the community where there were sick who needed us. We spent
the remainder of the Sabbath and other days to come
treating the ill in this area.

We knew then, in those beginning days, the need. There
were no doctors for hundreds of miles. Aside from our
medicines, which were given free, as were our treatments,
the only medical supplies were a few brought in by boat
and sold at prices most of the people could not afford. We
knew that we had to get more medicines and further medical training to help these people to better health. You
can't preach to people too sick even to listen.

So began our medical mission. On our second trip we
had a much larger supply of medicines to fight the plagues
of the river, and ultimately we made hundreds of trips
and treated ten of thousands of people.

Our journeys often lasted for many months. Our boat
was not merely a boat, it was our home, in many respects
perhaps more so than any house we had lived in before.
It was also our clinic, our consulting room, and our counseling office for people as beset with emotional problems
and worries and personality clashes as those in a more
civilized world. By her counsel, Jessie helped to save many
a marriage and kept many a home from smashing up.

Many of our experiences were heart-rending, but there
was also laughter and fun, and adventure enough. Our boat
boys, who helped with the cooking and the chores and the
details of boat operation, were always providing the unex-

pected note. We had all kinds of them over the years—good and bad, those with experience and those without, some who seemed able to cope with any emergency and others who could be depended on to do the wrong thing at the wrong time.

Our very first boy was a bright-eyed Indian who managed to get in the way of a small-time revolution later on, and was shot by government troops.

There was also John, known as our reluctant bridegroom because for years he warded off marriage to a young lady to whom he had proposed. She insisted they were betrothed, and so did her family. After four years of stalling, John found himself trapped. In the city of Manaus, Jessie helped him choose the bridal outfit, and the marriage went off with an elaborate ceremony, followed by a brief honeymoon on our boat. That was the end of John's carefree life on the river.

Another boy had come to our boat fresh out of the backwoods of the jungle. One night I asked him to take the wheel for a few moments while I rested. "Be careful," I warned him, "don't run us into the banks." We were making good time with the tide, doing about seventeen knots. Suddenly there was a terrible crash; we had run directly into the bank and only the fact that the river was high and the bank heavily wooded, so that the branches acted as a cushion, kept us from ripping apart. As it was, there was only minor damage and a startled boat boy who seemed to have no idea how it could have happened. "Maybe the bank hit us," he suggested.

Later on, foolishly, I asked him to take over in midstream, where we were comparatively safe from charging banks. I pointed to a star. "All you have to do is steer by that star," I told him. "Don't take your eye off it and nothing can go wrong."

"Yes, Senhor Leo," he said. "Don't worry."

After about half an hour, he called out. "Senhor Leo, Senhor Leo, I need your help!"

I hurried back. The boy was standing worriedly at the wheel. "I passed that star already," he said. "So could you give me another one?"

I looked outside. We were completely turned around and heading rapidly in the wrong direction.

The *Luzeiro* was crowded when another boy tried to light the stove and almost blew us up—people, boat, and all. The kerosene caught fire and the entire galley and engine room were swept with flames. I got the people off the boat, ran back with a quilt and threw it over the stove, and then picked up the stove and threw it and the quilt into the river.

By this time, however, I was overcome with fumes and collapsed on top of the motor. At that time the flywheel was not encased and it was turning at about 1,500 times a minute as my knee struck against it.

In the excitement I felt nothing, but when the fire was out and things had calmed down, I noticed that there was blood on my leg. The flywheel had cut it through to the bone. Jessie staunched the bleeding and gave me first aid. In the morning we reached a city where we obtained elementary medical care—these were the days before we ourselves had the latest medical equipment right on the boat. The gash was sewed up tidily, without anesthetic, with an ordinary needle and thread, while I gritted my teeth to keep from screaming with the pain. From that

time on, we were careful to keep inexperienced boat boys
away from stove and matches.

As years passed, the importance of our work along the
river increased. As the people came to depend on us, the
services which our church rendered were many and complex, and administrative work became more and more of
a problem.

More boats were needed, and more people. It became
part of my job to direct the building and operation of these
additional craft. The people came largely from our local
missions. In 1942, we built the *Luzeiro II*, which was of
the same design as the first but slightly larger. Jessie and
I took over and turned over the first for other missionary
work. Later, after the war, came *Luzeiros III* and *IV*, and
a number of smaller boats which we used for local work.

With this growing fleet we were reaching out into other
rivers in other areas of South America—the world above
Manaus, the world of Peru and Bolivia. One of our boats
also covered the San Francisco River in Baía. In 1955, we
built a small boat called the *Sentinela* for use by our book-
selling evangelists. By 1958, we had twelve boats scattered
over South America.

Other craft which look very much like ours also began
plying the Amazon. During World War II, when the Americans came to Brazil to try to build up the country's rubber production, they built eight boats patterned on my
design and used them as they worked, up and down the
river, to improve health conditions among the workers.

Materials of all kinds got scarcer and scarcer, and I
spent a good deal of my time scrounging for things we
desperately needed.

In Belém there were a number of American officials in

the main office of the rubber-development program, and one day I sailed the *Luzeiro* around to their headquarters to see if I could pick up some equipment.

As we pulled up to the dock, a well-dressed American came up to me and asked, "Where'd you get that boat?"

I told him I built it myself. The man said, "I'd like to buy it. How much do you want for it?"

I said that it wasn't for sale. Then I explained that we were members of the Adventist organization and rather than sell our boats we wanted to build more if we could only get the motors. The man, whose name, I learned, was Hines, looked at me oddly and said, "What kind of motors?"

"Any kind I can get."

"Well," he said, "I have three ten-horsepower outboard Johnson motors. If you want them, you can have them."

Want them! I could hardly believe it. I did my best to thank him, and later we invited him to have dinner on board with us. Jessie outdid herself that night in preparing an especially delicious Brazilian dinner. She was as grateful as I—and maybe even more curious as to why he had suddenly given us those motors, just like that.

She did not dare ask him outright, of course. But as the evening went on Mr. Hines began to tell us of his background. He had worked for the Goodyear people in Africa, he said, and while they were there his wife had been taken ill and needed an immediate operation. They were in the middle of the African wilderness and the only civilized help available was an Adventist mission—where there was an American doctor.

"We rushed my wife over to this mission by car—and the doctor saved her life. Since then I've always had a warm spot in my heart for your missionaries and their work. I could never thank them enough."

Every year we set out in February for the journey upriver from which we would not return until August. This, we found, was the best time of year, as the river reached flood stage in May or June and there was plenty of water to reach every home where we might be needed. At that time the river may rise as much as sixty feet. And the winds coming in from the Atlantic and sweeping upriver were not so strong or dangerous as at other seasons of the year. The tidal basin runs for several hundred miles up the river. The *pororóca* or moon-tidal wave of twelve to sixteen feet sweeps up the river at least once a month.

Making preparations for one of these trips was a protracted undertaking. The boat had to be outfitted, and the bottom of the hull painted in copper or arsenic paint to protect it from the bore that eats into the planking and causes serious damage. Then came the supplies. We made lists which we checked and rechecked endlessly, for if we forgot anything we might have to do without it for a long, long time. Our first consideration, in our later trips, was medicine and here we always had the help of our church people in gathering and wrapping and storing the vital supplies.

Groceries, linen—the housekeeping side of things—were largely in the hands of my wonderful wife and our boat girl, Irene. However, particularly in the early years, buying groceries in Belém for a long journey was not quite the same as shopping in a supermarket back in America. Fresh foods and fruit and vegetables we could obtain along the way. But we had to settle for substitutes for many of the familiar manufactured foods and cereals.

Finally, when everything was in readiness, our helpers would bring our luggage and supplies on down to the boat—usually carrying most of it on their heads—and medicines and personal baggage and perhaps some new article of furniture we had bought in Belém would all go on board. Then we would go around to the fuel dock to take on iron drums of oil—758 gallons in all. This was kept in our fuel tank or in the drums attached underneath our boat.

So we would start up a river that had become as familiar to us as the street outside our house in Belém. Within an hour the skyline of the city would disappear as we rounded Parrot Island, and the sound of our motor would be almost drowned out by the screeches of the birds for which it was named. They would fly in pairs, hundreds of them, as we passed, making an incredible din with their shrill cries.

We knew all the perils—the floating logs, some just below the surface where they could easily rip our boat apart; the alligators, as plentiful in our early years as the mosquitoes and still a navigational hazard; the tricky currents and the rocks awaiting a careless or untried pilot.

We had learned short cuts. Up a side river out of Belém is a canal dug by slave labor a hundred years ago. That saved us from having to cross the hazardous stretch of the Marajó Bay.

We knew the ways of the river and of travel. Upstream, we would hug the shore, where we could hear the shrill cries of bright-plumaged araras as they flew back and forth among the tall palms. Downstream with the current, like the river folk, we would go farther out, toward midstream.

We crossed wherever possible at the narrowest spots; knew that crossings from south to north can be difficult and dangerous; and that in a small boat such as ours it's often impossible to make headway against the currents.

We learned to trust in the protection of the Lord. An anchor chain breaks on a night when I am away, and Jessie wakens to find the boat swinging giddily among the other small craft in the harbor. But she and the boat boy get the motor started and so bring the *Luzeiro* under control and guide her safely to where she can be tied up at the dock. A rudder nearly breaks off—but holds, virtually by a thread, until we are safely across a dangerous place.

One year we had both the *Luzeiros I* and *II* at our annual camp meeting in Maués. The people were hungry for festivals and get-togethers, and we tried to satisfy this desire. On this occasion we had anchored the two little boats together, side by side, and the director of one of our missions had stretched canvas across the two boats to make shade for those waiting to have their teeth pulled, or cleaned, or filled, as required. Our boat—the *Luzeiro II* —was filled that day with sick who came to be treated, including quite a few of our followers. Those who had come to the meeting were getting injections of quinine along with the people of the area.

The five-year-old son of one of the directors was climbing around the boat when suddenly I heard a splash. Johnny had tumbled in. It was a moment of terror, for the waters were filled with instant death. The electric eel can stun and cause death by drowning—I recall an instance where thirty-four head of cattle were drowned in this way on one plantation before their owner discovered it was an eel at work. The deadly piranha was there in large numbers—this is a little fish with teeth so sharp they can tear a man to a skeleton in a matter of a minute or two. There were entangling vines and roots and swirling debris and logs and the killer alligators.

But the boat boy heard the splash, too. All dressed up in white linen for the evening meeting, he plunged in to save the boy. The child's father dove in a second later, but our boat boy had reached little John and brought him, dripping and frightened, back to the boat.

On one of our early trips we had to cross a fifteen-mile stretch of the Amazon, a journey that usually took about an hour. It was at floodtime, when the rains come and in the Andes the snows melt and rush down the streams feeding into this continental riverway. The river rises rapidly and the currents swirl on toward the sea, uprooting hundreds of trees along the banks. Some of them, like the itatuba, are so hard that they are heavier than water and sink to the bottom. Others float just under the surface, making them hard to see—and dangerous.

On that particular crossing we struck one of these submerged logs right in the middle of the wide river, where the current is at its most dangerous. We had no lifeboat with us, not even life jackets. There we were in the middle of the river with a huge gaping hole in the bottom and our boat rapidly filling with water.

Instinctively we sent up a prayer. I saw a long roll of canvas about a yard and a half wide. I had left this on top of the boat to dry. I felt impelled to unroll it. While I held one end and the boat boy the other, we passed it over the bow of the boat and underneath the bottom, working it back until we got to the place where the water was pouring into the gaping gash. As the canvas came near the hole, the pressure of the water forced it against the hole like a stopper in a sink, and no more water could enter. We were able then to make temporary repairs on the inside with wood and canvas, and to bail out the water that had poured in up to the floor of the boat.

And we thanked the Lord that He had inspired us to use that canvas.

I was the captain of my boat, licensed as such under Brazilian law. Later, in 1937, a measure was passed that only citizens of that country could have licenses to captain any kind of boat or ship. But because of the work we had done and were doing, and because I already had my credentials in any event, an exception was made in my case.

On our other boats, however, as our fleet of "mercy craft" expanded throughout the Amazon and Brazil and later into other South American countries, we used nationals as captains.

In many parts of Brazil the rivers are still the chief means of communication, and one of the responsibilities of little boats and their owners and operators is to serve as messengers and delivery boys and postmen all along the river. If we were going to a city or to some other place, we always asked if we could do anyone a favor—carry a parcel, mail a letter, make a purchase, or get something repaired. Many times we traveled with collections of alarm clocks and watches to be fixed, umbrellas to be repaired, and letters to deliver. Often we would spend a whole day in a city—running around delivering letters.

One item in demand was shoes. Many of the people along the river had no idea what size shoe they wore but they would give us a piece of paper torn to fit their foot, and when we reached a city like Manaus we would hunt for a pair of shoes that size.

In addition to carrying "unofficial" mail for friends, all boats along the river were required to carry the mail officially as well. We had to report to the post office in each community and tell them where we planned to go next and our estimated time of departure. If there was a mail sack for that port, we had to take it along; whether there was or not, we had to get a pass before we left, stating what mail, if any, we were carrying. Once, when leaving the town of Santarém, I forgot to get the pass. At our next port of call—Alenquer—I was placed under arrest by the local authorities because I did not have my pass.

I got word to the mayor of my plight. He interceded in my behalf and sent a wire to Santarém asking if I had taken any mail. When the reply came back in the negative, I was released. This was the only time I was arrested and the closest I ever came to spending the night in a tropical lockup.

Through this incident, however, the mayor, who was also a doctor, became a good friend. On our next visit he read the Bible with us and shortly thereafter he and his wife came to one of our meetings in Santarém and he announced that he was giving up his job as mayor to become an Adventist medical missionary.

After a three-year course at our college in São Paulo, he became director of our hospital in the Brazilian state of Mato Grosso, devoted to fighting the terrible disease known as "wildfire"—a rash that covers the whole body and burns like fire itself. He is now both doctor and minister.

Being arrested was a small price to pay for such an outcome as this.

The logbook was mainly sketchy jottings to keep a record of where we went. Yet for us these notes are a sample pattern of our lives:

"January 17. Left Cuno at 12:00 Ran to Lauro. Canoe leaked. Stopped many times to bail out water. Lots of rain. Got into Lauro at 6:00. Stopped for night at 7:00. Run in all 7½ hours."

"February 18. Tied up at bridge and a woman came and asked for medicine. Then asked us to go to her home to see boy with cancer. We went across river and about one kilometer down-river to their home. The man is a member of the Pentacostal church. The boy is about fourteen years of age. His right knee very much swollen but no pain. We treated him with penicillin and left ten injections for him to take. The tide turned about 11:30. We went on up-river. . . .

"September 3. Sabbath. Had Sab. school and in afternoon baptized seven souls. . . ."

CHAPTER 7

HYPOS AND HERONS

MEDICALLY speaking, the world of the Amazon was one of primitive ideas, superstitions, and practices. Disease was rampant. There were few or no doctors to be found in areas covering hundreds of miles; in some of the larger cities there were hospitals, but most of these were antiquated and outmoded. In the Amazon Valley, medical care was a luxury available chiefly to those aboard the ocean steamers heading up from Belém to Iquitos in Peru, with their tourist passengers lining the decks to gawk down at the natives along the riverbanks.

The travelers and the river folk were truly worlds apart. When one of the native Indian women has a baby, she simply squats down on the ground and the child is born, then she gets up, takes the baby down to the river to give it a bath, and goes back to her work. It is the prospective father who apparently goes through the greatest ordeal. At the time of the birth—I have actually seen this a number of times—the father wraps a white towel around his head, gets in his hammock, and stays there for two days.

The Indian women did not and in most cases still do not have a midwife or medical care of any kind before or during childbirth. The midwives who do work along the river are usually wildly superstitious; they are also usually dirty. They will arrive with a pair of dirty scissors which they use to cut the umbilical cord. Then the shears are put under the mother's bed, where they must stay. Once, when Jessie picked up the scissors, the midwife was furious and told her that the baby would have an infection and die because of what my wife had done. (It didn't.)

There are as many superstitions as there are diseases. Some of them go back to folk ideas found in lands all over the earth for hundreds, even thousands, of years past. They can be mighty unpleasant in the twentieth century. In one better-class family, one of the children had an attack of asthma. The mother got one of the boys out on a horse and made him ride it back and forth at a gallop until the animal was covered with lather. Then she took a table knife and scraped the lather off the horse. That was the medicine—taken internally—for asthma.

In cases of measles along the Amazon, members of the victim's family would be—and still are—sent out to follow a dog around until they could get some of the droppings. Of this they would make a tea which then would be given to the children to drink.

One of our workers called in a midwife in Manaus to deliver his wife's baby. The new mother noticed that the midwife was cooking something and when the midwife began to feed spoonfuls of the brew to the newborn infant, the mother asked what it was. "Oh, this is a tea I made out of cockroaches," the midwife told her. "It will make the cord fall off much faster."

The horrified mother got her child off this unsavory diet in a hurry!

One of our friends told us of a boy whose lower jaw had become infected after having been fed this tea. The jawbone was in such bad shape that the doctor was able to lift it out. He put it in alcohol, cleaned the boy up and sent him home. The mother returned, furious, and this so-called "doctor" said, "Well, all right, I will put the jawbone back if you so desire."

Within a few days this boy died.

In some of the wilder areas, the techniques of treating snakebite still involve the "charring" of the bitten area over an open fire. This is one of the most painful treatments ever dreamed up by man but, if the patient survives the shock, the method does seem to neutralize the poison. Many times we saw people along the Amazon with missing limbs; it is often because they underwent this treatment. The need for doctors on the river was obvious and urgent; for many did not want to come to an area where there were few paying patients and virtually no modern facilities and technical laboratories.

There are, of course, many snakebite cures sold in Brazil, as there were in the old days of the West. Printed right on the label of one of the most widely sold remedies is the legend about how it was discovered. The developer's goat was bitten by a deadly snake, the story goes, but ran off into the woods, ate of a shrub, and suffered no ill effects from the bite. The next time the goat was bitten, its owner followed it to the bush and when the goat again recovered from the bite, the man realized that he had something. He at once began to brew a medicine out of this shrub, and his secret elixir—by which, it is claimed, thousands have been saved—is sold all over Brazil.

We didn't know much about tropical diseases and our remedies were few and scanty, but they were a vast improvement on cures compounded of old wives' tales and witch doctors' incantations.

The principal diseases we encountered were malaria, yaws, tropical ulcers, cancers, hookworm, and other tropical infections. The people do not plant their food; for the most part they simply eat what grows in the woods, and their diet is not usually properly balanced.

Malaria fever was the terrible killer we had to deal with first. The two types most prevalent along the river were the Vivax or tertian type and the Falcifurium or malignant type. The former comes in violent attacks every other day; the latter comes every day and can be fatal in a few days, but if treated properly it can be arrested and does not need to recur.

There were times, during our first years, when almost everyone along the river had one or the other. I remember one village where every single person was ill with it. Everything in the town was closed up; it was like a village of the dead.

Dogs were barking and somewhere in this straw-roofed world I could hear a baby crying. We found the house from which the sound was coming and called but got no answer. When we pushed back the straw mat that hung over the door, we saw a terrible sight. The hammocks were filled, and other people were lying on the floor. They were all dead.

The only living thing in this house was a five-month-old baby; it lay in a hammock at the side of its dead mother. We got it out of the house and into the care of a good family, and the youngster has grown up without knowing anything of that tragedy or how close death was in that terrible hour of epidemic.

Another child in the same village, a ten-year-old girl who was also suffering from malaria, told us how her mother, father, and older brother had died. There was no one left to bury them, so the girl, weak as she was, had dug shallow graves and dragged the bodies of her family into them. She had scarcely crawled back to the house when a dog had come, rooted up the bodies, and began dragging them back and forth in front of the hut.

If these things sound shocking, it is because this was a shocking world and a shocking set of conditions we faced. These people, who were dying and helpless, were human beings whom we had come to help and to save, and we knew that we could not help them or save them spiritually until we could help them physically.

When we got back to Belém after our first trip and told other officials of what we had seen, everyone agreed that we should throw ourselves into medical work as quickly as possible. Jessie, of course, was a trained nurse and had a good grounding in medicine. I was an electrician turned minister. But the moment we reached Belém again we began our "medical courses" by getting hold of every available book on tropical medicine. The one I found most helpful was a volume published in Africa called *Medical Handbook for Tropical Diseases*. Written in layman's language, it was at the same time accurate and precise as to treatment. We were never without it on our launch from that time on.

In Belém we not only studied medicine, we began to gather up medical supplies on a sizable scale. We wanted all the equipment and medicines we could get. Some we bought out of mission funds, some were gifts, and some were wheedled from the Brazilian government. Our church, which had grown tremendously, helped us.

Many nights in Belém the members of our young people's organization would gather for a "Medicine Wrapping Night," sitting around the table and filling capsules with quinine—literally thousands of them—while others would measure out doses of Epsom salts. We used different colored papers—red, blue, yellow, and white—to indicate the size of the doses. These would be arranged in boxes, so that when we were treating a patient we could just reach into a box and pull out a dose of the proper size.

I learned a great deal about medicine as a result of these years when Jessie and I were literally the only medical help thousands of people had for thousands of miles. I did because I had to do; we did because there was nothing else to do; we learned because we had to learn in order to help them. We are not surgeons, but we operated when there was no one else at hand to try to save a life. We are not chemists, but we performed some chemical analyses. We did whatever a doctor does. In later years, the scope of our work broadened. We had considerable medical training in the Adventist Hospital and Medical Center in California.

It had not been planned for us to do this medical work; we had gone to the Amazon for a totally different purpose. But we had found a need and it had to be met.

There is no time in the jungle for debating the ethics of the medical profession. Here is a man who goes into the woods to cut rubber. A bushmaster snake attacks him. He lifts his large knife and slashes the snake in two, even as it is springing. But the part with the head and fangs continues its forward thrust and strikes him near the heart. Before we can get to him, the man is dead. The case might well stand as a symbol of the emergency—the immediacy of needs—wherever we turned.

During our first trips the only treatment we had for malaria was quinine. In recent years, for the most part we have used three modern medicines—Camequin, Aralem, and Daraprein. Just a few of these pills are sufficient to arrest malaria. Modern drugs—and an awareness of the need of these people—have changed the whole pattern of this disease. Many people have helped: the Brazilian government, American medical teams during the war, and the scientists who have developed the new drugs. A recent survey of three hundred residents of one Amazon district disclosed that, while all had had malaria, none had experienced a recurrence of it for five years. This does not mean that it has been eliminated; it does mean that strides have been made toward its control.

Perhaps in second place among the tropical diseases of the river is hookworm. Not a killer, it is almost as bad, for it saps the strength and makes the individual indolent and without ambition. The result is the kind of poverty and empty despair we found in so many of the districts we visited.

Hookworm is contracted by going barefoot, which many people in Brazil have done for centuries and continue to do. It is carried by a tiny, microscopic worm that gets in at the bottom of the feet and works its way up to the stomach, where it develops. Failure to dig proper sanitary facilities is responsible for the spread of the disease, which we found prevalent in Western Baía as well as in the Amazon areas.

One of our first jobs was to teach the people to dig

toilets, which must be done in order to control hookworm. Now, Brazil's public-health officials supply seats made of cement for these toilets and give them to the public in these districts. In addition, animated cartoon movies are shown to impress on the people's minds the importance of owning toilets.

Yaws, too, was one of the terrible diseases we found wherever we went. We saw hundreds of people, natives and Indians and nationals of varied blood, with sores all over their bodies, on their limbs, their feet, their hands, and sometimes even on their faces. We were in places where whole families, parents and children alike, lay helpless in their hammocks because the sores on their feet were so terrible they couldn't stand. Some of them had been prisoners of their hammocks for as long as three years, yet with a few injections of penicillin they were up and around again.

There are other infections and tropical ulcers, however, which are not so easy to cure. One of them is trachoma, which attacks the eyes. Brought to the Amazon many years ago by migrating Japanese, it spreads like wildfire in a country that might have been made to order for it. People who used common towels in public restaurants, drank from communal cups, and in general lived under poor sanitary conditions spread trachoma widely along the Amazon. Then, because it was usually not properly treated, it brought on blindness.

One night we were holding a dedication service in the large top-floor room of one of the few three-story houses along the river. Just as the meeting was breaking up, I looked out across the stream in the beautiful moonlit night and saw four men paddling across it in our direction in a

large canoe. When they were close enough, they called up
to me from their boat and asked if I was Senhor Leo. They
had been sent, they told me, by a man named Cornelius.
"What does he want?" I asked.

"He and his family are all sick. They have sore eyes.
They are in terrible pain. They want you to come over
and treat them."

It was late, so I told them that I would leave early in
the morning and be there by daybreak. They insisted on
staying so that they could direct me; they hung up their
hammocks in the big house and went off to sleep. Early
next morning, we piloted the *Luzeiro* across the river,
around some islands, and into another beautiful stream.
It was a place of flame-colored birds and, a little farther
along, herons—great white crowds of them ahead of us in
flight.

At last we reached the home of Cornelius. A successful dealer in rubber and other products along the Amazon,
he apologized to Jessie and me for having disturbed us
and making us come so far. "But we are sick and we do not
know what to do," he added. "Some of us are now almost
blind."

We hadn't had much experience in treating eye trouble,
so we prayed for special guidance in this case. Then we
examined all these people and found that they all had
what appeared to us to be trachoma. The best drug we
had available to treat this, we figured, was sulfathiazole,
so we counted out sixty of these pills for each man, gave
them all instructions about the proper dosage, and Jessie
warned them, "As soon as you can, get down to the city
to an eye specialist or you may lose your sight entirely.
Do you all understand me?"

Jessie's tone was firm but her brown eyes were gentle. Our patients, impressed, we thought, assured us they would follow our advice in every respect, thanked us profusely, and stood waving on the dock as we pulled away.

Four months later, on our return trip, I stopped to hold another religious meeting in the three-story house and again, as we were finishing, I looked out and saw four men drawing near in their boat. Once again they said that Cornelius had sent them. "What's the matter now?" I asked. "Didn't they go to town and have their eyes treated?"

"Oh, they are all well now; they have no trouble with their eyes any more. They want you to come over and have a praise meeting to give thanks." The spokesman smiled. "They didn't go to any specialist; it was your pills that did it."

So once again the white *Luzeiro* crossed the river, passed the islands, and tied up at Cornelius's dock. While I set up our projector and showed a motion picture, the first they had ever seen, Jessie, who had seen it many times before, wandered into another room. There she found four women. "Why aren't you watching the movie?" she asked.

"We can hardly see," one of the women answered. "When you were here you treated the others but not us." This time, as Jessie hustled about handing out sulfathiazole pills, we didn't have to wonder whether we were doing the right thing. We had talked, meanwhile, to eye specialists and learned that this is the exact drug they use for trachoma. One of them had told us, "By giving them that drug, you may have saved them from lifelong blindness."

Even in the far back streams of the Amazon, word gets

around fast, and people always managed to get word to us when they needed us. When they were expecting a baby, they usually let us know well in advance. Of course, obstetrics was Jessie's special department.

On one case we had run all night long to get to an expectant mother in time. Jessie, in her crisp white nurse's uniform, was busy inside with the woman while the father-to-be and I were waiting on the deck of the boat. "Have you thought of any name for your baby yet?" I asked.

"Oh yes, we have a wonderful name," the man answered. "We are going to call him Franklin Delano Roosevelt."

"Well, that's a fine name," I said.

As we were talking, Jessie came out of the house with the new baby in her arms, "I'm afraid," she laughed, "you'll have to call this one Eleanor."

The obstetrical cases were sometimes difficult, and Jessie was fortunate, often, to save the mother. In one instance, the family waited nearly four hours to tell her the birth had been complicated; the child had arrived but not the placenta. Jessie successfully delivered the after-birth even in this case.

Many of the complications arose out of plain ignorance or superstition and lack of facilities. Sanitary conditions such as are required in the most rudimentary hospitals were completely lacking in almost every instance. Yet my wife carried off these hundreds of cases successfully.

The malaria and the hookworm and the yaws were bad enough in our early years, but what hit us hardest, I think, were the terrible injuries from alligator attacks. I recall one case of twins, each of whom lost a leg to an alligator. They used to joke about their plight, saying that since they wore the same size shoe and one had lost a left and the other a right leg, "We only need one pair of shoes." Somehow it never seemed very funny to me.

Not too untypical was the case of Rachel, the oldest of a family of twelve children living along the river. She had gone one day to the bathhouse, which all Amazon families have in front of their homes. As she washed some clothes, a huge alligator came along and grabbed Rachel by the hips. Fortunately, its underjaw caught in a board under the bathhouse and, when it tried to pull the little girl into the water, it found it couldn't without pulling in the whole building as well. This was impossible, even for such a huge creature.

While it threshed about in the stream, one of her brothers heard her screams and came running. As he began to hit the alligator over the head with a club, it made one last effort to pull the girl in. It failed and finally its teeth pulled away, tearing all the flesh on the girl's thigh.

When we got there the next day, we patched up Rachel's terrible wounds as best we could and gave her an injection of penicillin. Happily, she recovered without infection developing.

Accidents of this sort, which seemed so horrible to us, were commonplace to a people who lived close to violence and even savagery and certainly to the cruelty of nature. They grew used to it, and accustomed, too, to their own courage in the face of these dangers.

A little woman came to our boat one day to tell us her story, although she knew we could do nothing about the empty sleeve which dangled from one thin shoulder. One night, she said, she was asleep in her hammock when, suddenly, she was awakened by the shrill screams of her baby. She got up quickly and lit the kerosene lamp.

"There by the flame I saw my baby with its arm in a big alligator's mouth. I didn't know what to do, but I prayed for God's help. Then I was impressed to pick up one of those long poles used in our fireplaces. It was red-hot at one end—and I put that in the alligator's mouth just beside where it held the baby's arm. The alligator made a terrible sound and opened its mouth, and I was able to grab my baby away.

"But as I reached down to pick up my baby, the alligator gave a lunge and grabbed me by the right arm, at the shoulder. Then it started to carry me out to the river. When it was trying to pull me through the door, I prayed again for strength. I reached out with my left hand and caught the door post, and it could not get me through. So it gave a mighty jerk to dislodge my hold and tore off my arm. It bled terribly, but, fortunately, neighbors came. They have an outboard motor on their canoe and took me to the city, and there the doctor fixed up my arm and saved my life."

"Where did you ever find the courage to struggle with that creature?" we asked her.

"I forgot myself," the woman said. "My one thought was to save my baby."

Many times we saw examples of this sort of valor—in the boys who had lost their legs to a ferocious twenty-two-foot alligator; in this woman who had saved her infant. Or in the case of one elderly lady whose daughter was ill in bed.

It was floodtime and the water was well over the river-banks when we came up in front of the house where the elderly woman lived. There was a stream about a foot deep flowing right through her house, and we could maneuver our boat to within about ten feet of her door. She stood there in the water, crying out that her daughter was sick and could we please do something to help. "How can we get in?" I shouted. "We can't get our boat in any closer."

"Just stay there—can you hold the boat there?"

I said we could. The old woman said, "Wait, please."

The frail old woman turned then and went into the house. In a few minutes she appeared again at the door, carrying in her arms her daughter, a girl much bigger and heavier than the mother. Before Jessie and I realized what she was doing, she was wading into the water, lifting the girl into our boat, and climbing in herself.

We carried the girl into the cabin and found on examination that she had malaria. We gave her a quinine injection, and supplied the mother with medicine to give her daughter until the fever subsided.

The mother's beaming smile of gratitude more than repaid us. We helped her get the daughter back into a hammock in the partially flooded house, and went on about our work, warmed in spite of our water-drenched clothes.

So the work we did developed and reached out to more and more people. Despite the drama of individual cases, the main element of our program lay in training the people to be aware of their own medical needs. This plan eventually led to the organization of clinics and hospitals—a later phase of our work and our story—and to the unfolding program of our launches and their operators. Most of these latter were not foreign missionaries like us, but nationals.

It was our idea that Brazilians should take over this work wherever possible; they did not need outsiders, once they had learned.

Many of the people with whom we dealt had no idea of medicine or what it was for, in those beginning days when we pioneered along the river. Scores of these folk were terrified of our treatment and wanted to stay with the old ways, even though these meant continued sickness, pain, hopelessness, and death.

We had to teach the basic principles of hygiene before we could begin to make headway. Hundreds of times I have watched Jessie, clean and shining in her white uniform, talking pregnancy and childbirth and infant care to a group of women to whom modern medicine was as mysterious as the atom bomb.

Jessie held cooking classes for the Brazilian housewives along the Amazon. There was more to these lessons than a new way to cook sweet potatoes. She was able, in this way, to introduce new ideas of hygiene in cooking. Much of what we taught at the beginning was elementary—the need for proper sanitation and cleanliness and for taking care of the teeth. All of this was part of the early preventive program we introduced. Later, working with Brazilian health officials, we assisted in expanding this program over wide sections of the country.

As our work progressed and we became better known, the people of these isolated communities would be waiting for us when our boat dropped anchor. Their sick would come to our clinics on the *Luzeiro*, case after case. Often there would be long lines of these people, waiting their turn. Many times we would inoculate a whole community against smallpox or some other disease if there was danger of an epidemic.

Some of the cases we treated had their humorous overtones. One day a black-bearded man came aboard. "Captain, is it all right for me to shave now?" he asked.

"Why haven't you been shaving?"

"Well, I didn't think I was supposed to. I took castor oil two weeks ago."

I recall another instance that occurred during one of our improvised clinics on the boat. We had arrived late at a community quite far up the river, but there were many persons waiting to be treated. One was a man who had brought his twelve-year-old son for us to look over. "I don't know what's wrong with him—he eats dirt and sand and everything," the man said.

Jessie examined the boy and then told the father, "This boy has hookworm, that's all." She gave him a remedy for this disease, which we always carried, in a healthy dose of castor oil. "See that he takes this at five o'clock tomorrow morning, on an empty stomach," she directed.

"I can't do that," the man said. "We don't have any alarm clock and how will I know the time?"

"Do you have a rooster?" Jessie asked.

"Of course."

"Well, when the rooster crows, give him the medicine."

He agreed to follow instructions, and several months later, when we stopped by again, we asked him how the boy was getting along. "Oh, he's fine now, completely cured," the father said. "But the rooster died, after we gave him that medicine like you said we should."

We spent many long days treating scores of patients and giving injections, while I perspired through shirt after shirt in the intense heat. For a long time I was hesitant about using the needle and would leave this to the more experienced hands of Jessie, although I would help her with the preparations and knew every detail of the procedure. I was perfectly capable of giving injections, but I kept finding excuses until one day Jessie simply left me alone with the patient and I had to do the job myself. I really sweated then, from nervousness, but the lad held out his arm and I hid my inner emotions and gave him the injection. When I finished, the boy's pal, who had been looking on, inquired eagerly, "Did it hurt?"

The youngster lifted his head disdainfully. "How could it hurt when it was given to me by an experienced man like Senhor Leo?"

Perversely, I suppose, this was to me one of the most important moments in all our years on the Amazon. From that moment on, I had no worries about giving injections. In a sense, I got my medical degree—I had it on the word of my patient.

As we went along on our trips up and down the river, almost every evening we would hold services, usually in some country store or village or farmhouse. (Many a so-called village is actually only a store to which people come from the surrounding area.) One evening we were to have a service in a home, but so many people came—close to three hundred—that we had to hold it outside, under a giant mango tree. We put up our wires, showed our films, sang hymns, and I gave the sermon. It was afterward that we were told of a terrible epidemic of smallpox not far away. Everyone present needed to be vaccinated, and we actually set up an assembly line that night. We had them all bare their right arms. As one of our helpers wiped each arm clean with alcohol, Jessie and I would put on the vaccine and scratch the arm. This way we were able to handle several hundred individuals in something less than an hour.

Even so, it was after eleven by the time we had treated the last person. Then we had to take down our wires and pack up our equipment and get it into the boat. As we shoved off, all three hundred people crowded around on the riverbank and asked us for one more song. So we stood there on the bow of our boat and sang the familiar, "God Be with You Till We Meet Again."

It was a deeply stirring moment. As our boat pulled away from the shore, we could hear a tremendous chorus across the night, "Come back soon . . . come back soon. . . ."

CHAPTER 8

BY ANOTHER WAY

THERE is elusive mystery in the world of the Amazon, where the witch doctors talk of powers that drift like green wraiths in the shadows of the palms. There is mystery in the cries of strange creatures, in the deepening of twilight and the dark fastnesses beyond which white man does not proceed. There is an eerie light in the black waters of the Rio Negro; there is enigma in the legend of Phoenician mariners centuries past sailing up the Solimões to find giant cedars for Solomon's Temple, and leaving his name behind, as the story insists, in the name of that river.

It was a world of dark forces, superstitions, appeals to the demoniac and the damned. We came with another purpose and another Power in whom we put our faith.

In Belém, after our first trip or two, we began to realize that medicine was expensive. The church could furnish some of the funds we needed to buy it, but our Amazon district was, after all, only one part of a world-wide organization and we could not expect more than our share of help from that source.

The governor of Pará, Colonel Jocquin Barata, however, was a friend of the Adventists and I went to him and told him of our need for medicines. "Oh," he said, "you go on over to our public-health people and tell them I said to give you anything you need. Draw up a list."

I did as he suggested. It was a long list and when I took it over to one of the public-health officials he looked at it, listened to my story of our work and the governor's state-ment, and said very definitely, "The state of Pará hasn't got enough medicine for our own medical posts here. We certainly haven't enough to furnish your needs, too. I'm sorry."

I went back to the governor, showed him the list, and told him how I had been turned down. Without a word he wrote out an order instructing the public-health officer to give me every single thing I needed.

I went back. I did not like having had to go over the man's head to his superior but I needed the supplies too desperately to let protocol stand in my way.

This time I gave him the note from the governor. He read it, asked for my list, and began to cross off items he said they "didn't have." When he was through, the only thing left unchecked was a supply of Epsom salts worth about two dollars.

The health official's tone was icy as he said, "Come back tomorrow, go to our supply department upstairs, and pick up your Epsom salts."

He had even struck off the quinine!

The next morning, before I went to get the Epsom salts, we had our usual prayer and reading and I took my prob-lem to God. Then I set out for the public-health offices.

When I got up to the supply department, I found a man sitting at a desk piled high with papers. I don't think I ever saw a desk piled so high or in such a clutter; he had to keep pushing the papers back to keep them from falling on the floor. He asked me what I wanted, and I explained that the medical official on the floor below had sent up an order for me to get some medicine. The man began to look for the requisition, but in the sea of papers it was obviously a hopeless task. Finally he said, "Well, what did you want, anyway, Mr. Halliwell? We're pretty well stocked."

From my pocket I took out a copy I had made of the list with all the things I wanted—and the note from the governor. He looked these over and said, "Sure, we've got all of it. You get over here this afternoon with a truck and we'll have it waiting."

My pickup truck and I were Johnny-on-the-spot that afternoon, and the kindly man was on hand to help me load up. He knew about our work and, as I drove off, he said, "Now, any time you run out of medicines anywhere in the state, just send me a telegram and I'll ship it right along."

From that time on, we had at least one main source of supply, although, of course, much more had to be bought in Rio or in the States. Even the official who had turned me down cold was extremely cordial and co-operative on my second visit some months later.

During the war we had a tremendous problem with quinine, which we needed constantly to combat malaria. The Japanese had cut off the major source of supply—the Far East—and we scraped and scrounged continuously for even small quantities.

This, too, was a problem we took to God. In Buenos Aires, not long after America came into World War II, I was giving a talk about our work on the Amazon, when a man named Williams asked me to visit him in his office when I was in town again. This I did. He was off visiting his copper mines, but he had told his secretary to talk to me. She wanted a few more facts about our work and our experiences, to report to him on his return.

Then she said, "Oh, by the way, Mr. Williams has some quinine for you that he thought you might need because of the shortage."

In a storeroom in the basement she pointed to a shelf crowded with packages wrapped in brown paper. "That is all quinine," she told me. "Ten kilos—about twenty-two pounds."

It was a vast supply for anyone to have at such a time and I was gazing at it longingly, thinking of how many people it would help, when she said, "Look closer, Mr. Halliwell." Then I saw that all the packages were marked, "Halliwell. To be used in Amazon."

In this time of need, when quinine was impossible to get, God had opened a way for me to obtain a supply that would serve the needs of hundreds on the river.

But if our work was truly a mixture of medicines and miracles, it was grounded in solid medical training, too. To Jessie's nursing course we added training we gave ourselves in Brazil, and studies in tropical medicine in our faith's hospitals in America, from which come some of the finest surgeons and physicians and nurses in the medical profession.

On our furlough to the States in 1936, we were privileged to study at the White Memorial Hospital, a part of the medical school at Loma Linda, California, where Jessie amazed the doctors by her ability to diagnose tropical diseases without a flicker of hesitation.

She was called into a clinic one day and shown a little

Mexican girl sitting on an observation table. "Now, Mrs. Halliwell," the doctor said, "I wish you would turn this girl around and tell us what you think she has."

Jessie looked the girl over carefully. "Well, up here in the States I wouldn't know the name they use," she said. "But in Brazil I would call this a form of leprosy."

This case had apparently been quite difficult to diagnose and the doctor was both startled and happy at her speed and accuracy.

We worked directly in the clinics, side by side with the doctors. We put special time into the study of skin diseases, so prevalent in the tropics, and Jessie took extra training in obstetrics. While she was doing that, I was working in the laboratory, learning how to analyze blood and other specimens. It was a sound basic training in "lab" technique, and later we had instruments on our boat so that we could make our own tests on the spot. In addition, from the very beginning, and particularly when we went back to the States on leave, we got hold of every book available on tropical diseases and their treatment. None of this seemed like work to us, for it was a subject which had become one of the main interests of our lives.

Of course, we were not the only ones to take these courses. Many of our boat captains have studied in our colleges and schools in Brazil, have worked in our hospitals in the south of the country, and as a result have a sound basic knowledge of the diseases which they have to deal with in their daily work.

We always worked closely with doctors and medical officials in Brazil, and often doctors would go with us on our trips, both to study our problems and the way we handled them and to assist in treating patients. Where a case was serious, we made every effort to get the patient to a hospital in Belém, or Manaus, or to a doctor if there was one not too far away. But too often there was no practicing physician for hundreds of miles—even after thirty years of our work and "educational" program.

This work of ours was a blend of medicine and faith, but it was also a constant war on superstition and ignorance. Of this we had many examples—from the man who wanted me to pour some of the light from the electric bulb into a bottle, so he could take it home to show his wife, to the mother who did not want us to cure her small son because his begging on the town streets was her sole source of support.

An ulcer had eaten away the whole top of this twelve-year-old's foot when we found him. I gave him an injection and some hot-and-cold-water applications, and told him to continue the treatments every day. To make it all seem more important to him—many of the people we dealt with could not believe that hydrotherapy had any value— I gave him some harmless potassium permanganate to color the water. But the boy had scarcely had time to get home when his mother arrived at the *Luzeiro*, puffing and angry. What did we mean, she asked furiously, by trying to cure her boy and thus do her out of her only means of livelihood? But there were times when we had to get tough, and this was one of them. I finally went to the civil authorities, who compelled the mother to let us treat her child.

He used his colored water faithfully after that and before many weeks he could run and play—and work—like other boys. When she discovered he was then able to earn more than he used to get by begging, his mother, I heard, was properly grateful.

But selfishness, such as this mother's, was not one of our worst enemies. Ignorance, superstition, prejudice against the new and untried—these were our real foes, as deadly often as the terrible bushmaster or the lunging alligator.

The night we set up an assembly line and vaccinated some three hundred people against smallpox, there was one man I especially wanted to inoculate—the old chief. He had said he would never let anyone puncture his arm and that nothing could make him change his mind.

A year later, when we were back in the same little river town, several people told us, "You had better go visit the old chief right away. He is sick and stretched out on a banana leaf."

(When they have fever, the Indians lie on a large banana leaf instead of in their hammocks; they say the leaf is cooler.)

I found the chief lying on his banana leaf, his body covered with smallpox from head to feet. "I am happy to see you, I am glad you have come," he said, putting both arms around me and giving me an Indian hug.

"Why? Is there something you want to see me about?"

"I want to be vaccinated," he said.

He said those five words with dignity, as if he were surrendering the most sacred traditions of his ancestors. Of course, he had made his fateful decision slightly too late, but the fact that he had made it was important. The word spread in the area. It was a symbol that the old days were gone. Fortunately, although he had a lasting reminder in his scars, the chief did recover.

As our work in the Amazon developed, our problems of administration grew, too. From that first day when we arrived in Belém to take over a "parish" that included the whole river—and a membership of three, all of whom were standing on the dock to greet us—the Amazon Mission finally reached such numbers that it had to be broken up. One section, with headquarters at Belém, included the lower Amazon. Another, the Central Amazon Mission, operated out of Manaus.

The man who helped me the most in getting this new organization under way was Walter Streithorst, who took over the central Amazon area with his wife Olga. It was she we had seen as an infant on her satin pillow at our first Sabbath service in Brazil. Her father, Pastor Storch, had worked in our church for many years, both in Baía and in the Amazon, and we had watched Olga as she grew up, as dear to us as one of our own.

Walter was a Brazilian national, born in Rio Grande de Sal. He had studied for a couple of years in Germany, from where his father had emigrated, and had finished his education in our Adventist college in São Paulo. He served in the Brazilian army during the war and took some courses in nursing and caring for the sick and wounded. He and Olga were married in 1943.

After the war, Walter became president of the Central Amazon Mission of our church organization, while I was in charge of the entire Northern Brazil Union, embracing the whole area. Eventually, Walter was to take over the Northern Union while I went south to be in charge of all boats and boat work in the South American division.

The thoroughness of missionary training is exemplified in Walter. Although he had a sound basic educational background to begin with, we sent him to the States for additional study, first to our medical training college in California, where he took courses in dentistry, and then to Washington, D.C., where he was enrolled at our seminary in business administration.

Walter and Olga were close friends of ours, and many times, particularly at special conclaves along the river, we would tie up our boats side by side at a port along the Amazon and hold what was almost a family reunion. They have two children, a wonderful boy and girl, and seeing them always reminded us of the days when our own children were young and with us in Belém and on that first trip up the river.

Thanks to men of this caliber and their families, mostly Brazilians but also some Americans, our work pushed forward. Conditions improved; diseases such as hookworm and malaria began to subside in the area; death from snakebite began to diminish. Even the alligators—possibly largely because they were being destroyed for commercial reasons—began to be less of a terror in the more populated regions. Yet there was still widespread sickness in some areas; when American officials began their rubber-development program during the war, they found disease still a major factor in delaying production.

Because of this, the Americans and Brazilians together, with America footing most of the costs, organized what was called the Serviço Especial de Saúde Público—the SESP or Special Public Health Service. These experts came to us to study our boat and our techniques, and ultimately built eight launches patterned after the *Luzeiro*. They also brought up to the river for the first time a number of doctors who, by law, had to be Brazilians. (In the past, Brazilian physicians had stayed away from the Amazon because they could not make a living among people who had no money; during the war emergency, they were paid by the government, and when the emergency ended, they returned to their regular practices.)

The principal reason for bringing in these doctors, organizing the SESP, and building these boats was to improve health conditions rapidly over a wide area so that the people could go out and cut the rubber America desperately needed. A Rubber Development Commission, with offices in Belém and Manaus, brought a number of boats and organized what was called a rubber bank. Anyone who had rubber trees could go to this outfit and get money to expand production. All of this activity brought a great boom along the river and hundreds of workers poured in, ready to go out and cut rubber. It was the new gold and diamonds and emeralds all in one.

Without question, the wartime influx of American workers and engineers, with their ideas of sanitation, changed and in many ways awakened the valley as nothing else had done. While the rubber was being taken down-river and—because of the number of Nazi submarines off the coast—flown out in giant planes, sanitary conditions were improved and malaria control was broadened as many mosquito-breeding areas were cleaned up.

Along with this came increased discoveries and developments in anti-snakebite serums from the remarkable "snake farm" and laboratory called Butantan in São Paulo. This was founded some years ago by Dr. Vitel Brasio, whose experiments with Brazil's twenty-two varieties of poisonous snakes have provided medicines which have saved thousands of lives. Many of these serums we have delivered to villages and communities in large enough supply to protect the people of the area. Wherever possible, it was our practice to leave enough medicines so that the people—nationals or Indians—could care for their own needs.

We did what we could wherever we went, even performing minor surgery if there was no doctor or hospital within reach. We had gone far up above Manaus—so far it would have taken days or weeks to get further medical help—when we encountered a native with a toe that had become terribly infected. Long before we could have got him out of the spider web of rivers in which he lived, the infection would have spread and he could well have died, as the toe was definitely gangrenous. We had the man brought into the boat, sterilized the surgical equipment which we carried for emergencies, and Jessie began the surgical operation with me assisting. For anesthetics we used Novocaine.

The amputation of a toe may not be a difficult operation under normal circumstances, but neither of us was a surgeon, and we were in the middle of the jungle without professional help or guidance. With a sureness that I think would have done a professional surgeon credit, Jessie disjointed the toe and removed it, cleaned away all the infection, bathed and bandaged the wound, and sent this man hobbling on his way with instructions for changing dressings and guarding against further infection.

I recall an incident that occurred not far from São Luis in the state of Maranhão. Olga's father, who was holding meetings there, announced one night that one of our boats was on hand and that on board was his assistant, a man named Americo Quispe, a fully trained "medic" or nurse, who would try to help any who needed him.

The first person to reach Quispe after the meeting was a frightened woman. "Please come to my house at once," she entreated him. "Two of my children are terribly ill. I don't know what to do to help them."

When they reached her house, scarcely more than a shack, on the edge of the city, he found the two children almost lifeless in their hammocks.

Examination told him that they were suffering from typhoid fever and were near death. "There is a specific drug for the typhoid—chloromycetin," he told her. "I have no more of these pills left on my boat or I would give you all you need free of charge. But they sell them here in the city, in the pharmacy, and you can buy all you need."

"How many will that be?" the mother asked.

"It will be expensive," he told her. "Each child will need about sixty pills, and they retail at about forty cents a pill."

Quispe didn't have to look in his pockets. He knew he had no money. He also knew it would take days to get the pills from one of our church officials hundreds of miles to the south.

The woman began to cry. She told him, "The pills may be able to save my children but we have no money to buy them. I can only sit here and watch my children die."

The young evangelist took her hand in his. "There is a God in Heaven who hears and answers prayers, and if you like we can bow down and ask Him now and He won't let these children die."

The woman nodded. They knelt down beside the hammocks, and the young man sent up a prayer of appeal for this woman and her children. Then he said good night.

All the way back into the city he pondered this problem. Perhaps Pastor Storch might have a little money. Maybe they could make up a pool of a few dollars here and there. Perhaps. . . .

As he passed the City Hall, a man stepped out of the shadows. "Aren't you the fellow on the little Adventist boat? The one with the medicines on board?"

Americo Quispe nodded. "I wish you would come with me now, this minute, up to my hotel room," the man said.

The evangelist was not eager to go. Luring people into hotel rooms was a familiar trick. The man might be planning to rob and kill him. Despite his doubt, he agreed to go.

As he unlocked the door and ushered Quispe inside, the man said, "I happen to be a salesman for the Lilly Laboratories in São Paulo. I heard your boat was here. A little while ago I felt impelled to go out and find you and make you a present of some pills I have here. Will you please accept them as a gift from me?"

He handed the startled young man a bottle containing a thousand chloromycetin tablets—the very drug needed so desperately for the children he had left only a few minutes before.

Tears came to Quispe's eyes as he told the story to us later: "I thanked him and bounded down those stairs three at a time. I went right straight back to that woman's home, gave the children their dosage, and counted out the pills she needed."

Within two weeks, these children, who had been in the very arms of death, were well.

But the incident that stands out most unforgettably for Jessie and me concerns a detour I had no intention of taking. We were in Manaus and were in a hurry to get downriver to Maués, where we were to hold a five-day old-fashioned "camp meeting." Four or five hundred of our church members were to be there.

On the way down we were stopped near the mouth of the Madeira River. Some people were sick—rubber cutters and their families. Even though we were pressed for time, we couldn't leave until we had treated them all. It was nearly four o'clock when we got under way.

From that point there were two routes we could take to Maués. One was up the Madeira River and down a narrow channel in Maués. The other was down the Amazon itself and then back up a narrow channel to the city. The latter was five or six hours shorter. As we started out, about to cross the mouth of the Madeira, Jessie asked me which route I proposed to take. "Well," I answered, "since time is pressing, we'll go by the Amazon."

Jessie wasn't too happy at my decision. "Just look at those storm clouds over there. We'll ride right into them."

I agreed. "Yes, we'll run the risk of a storm; but we've got all those people waiting, so we'll have to go this way."

We started down the Amazon, across the two-mile stretch of water at the mouth of the Madeira. I was sitting at the wheel and had tight hold of it to keep it going straight. When we reached the middle, something happened, something grabbed the wheel. I am a strong man, with heavy chest and shoulder muscles, and I tried to hold it, but I couldn't. Something stronger than I turned that wheel, and we started up the Madeira River.

I thought perhaps a log had caught under the rudder

and I peered over the side. I could see nothing. I tried to turn the wheel back in the direction of the Amazon. It wouldn't budge. For once, I was really afraid. Finally, I thought: Well, if this thing wants to go up the Madeira River—we'll go up the Madeira.

An instant later, Jessie came in. "What's the matter?" she asked. "What made you change course?"

I told her I didn't change it, but that something had prevented me from turning the wheel. "I'm glad," she said. "I was back there praying we would go this way, out of the storm, instead of on the Amazon."

As we kept on up the Madeira, the boat behaved perfectly normally. About ten o'clock, long after dark, we pulled into the narrow channel that goes down to Maués and we decided to stop for the night. Just as we dropped anchor, lightning flashed and a storm broke. The rain was like a roaring cascade around us and the winds blew at cyclonic force. On the wide Amazon, we almost certainly would have met disaster; but here in the narrow stream, we were safe.

All was calm the next morning. We started out early and about nine o'clock, as we rounded a bend in the stream, we saw a high bank, a house, and a man waving a white towel for us to stop. As we put down our gangplank to go ashore, the man—a Brazilian—said, "I'm awfully sorry to stop you, but my daughter is just about dead. Can you come and try to save her?"

When we reached the house, he pulled back the straw mat hung over the door and there we saw a young girl about nineteen lying in a hammock and groaning in pain. She was pretty and light skinned, her arm was wrapped up in an improvised tourniquet, a rag pulled around tightly with a stick, and the forearm was almost black. She had some kind of medicine on her hand—it looked like an "ointment" made of cow dung which people in the area often used.

Jessie took one look at the tourniquet, pulled out her scissors, and cut the bond. The father protested. "Oh, no— we put that on yesterday to keep the blood poisoning in her hand from going through her system."

Jessie paid no more attention to him than she would have to a fly. She was too busy trying to save his daughter's life. She began to heat water. She bathed the hand. She gave the girl a dose of penicillin and took off the layers of "medication." Then she treated the girl's hand with hot compresses of Epsom salts, and after some time we were able to open up the infected spot and drain off the pus. After a little while, the girl stopped groaning. Obviously she was feeling better. "I want to tell you a story now about this," she said.

She had been picking fruit and a thorn on one of the trees had stuck into her hand. It had become infected and as time went on the infection had become worse and worse. By the afternoon before, pain was shooting up her arm and down her side. As she lay in agony, a man had gone past the house. "There is a little boat in Maués," he told them, "a little white medical boat that goes along the river. I am sure if they should come down this river they could help you."

The girl—who later completely recovered—told us that after the man left she got out of her hammock and knelt down and prayed that this little white boat would come down the river. And she told her father to go out and wave a towel if any small white boat appeared.

I asked her what hour it was that she prayed.

"Oh, it was just a little after four yesterday afternoon," the girl said.

CHAPTER 9

LABYRINTHS IN GREEN

TO reach the Indians above Maués, you cross a
wide clear lake and enter a narrow stream. It is only thirty
or forty feet wide but very deep; the banks plunge almost
straight down and the water is black as night. In the morning, when there is no wind and no ripples, the water is like
a translucent blue-black gem, reflecting the dark green of
the jungle above, the giant Brazil-nut trees, towering above
all others in the jungle, and patches of blue sky. By this
route—it was not the same as that we took on our first trip
—we could go from this stream into the wide, slowly moving Andirá River. It, too, looks black but if you dip up a
cup it is as clear as water from a mountain spring.

Our first visit to these Indians took us up the Maués
River, but there are trails between the Maués and the
Andirá over which the Indians maintain communication.
They are all part of the same tribal group.

These Indians on the Andirá had had contact with white
people, but none had ever seen or heard a motor launch.
When they heard us approaching they all fled from the
village, but a little later they came back to see us. I took
a boxful of dry goods over to the shore, along with an old-
fashioned victrola, which I cranked up. A record of lively
music excited them and they crowded around the victrola

like children, so close I feared they would break it. To surprise them, I put on another record of a man singing in a strong tenor voice. When they heard *that* coming out of the box, they turned and fled back into the woods, leaving me alone on the shore with my victrola and some tenor singing the Brazilian national anthem. I took that record off and played some more band music, and I could see them peeking out around the trees. Finally, they began to come back, one by one.

This was on our second trip to this general area and I had brought along my projector and my film. I was very anxious to show this to the Indians. However, when I took the projector out of the box, they evidently thought it was a gun and turned once more and scuttled into the woods.

Once again I played a little more band music and once again, after considerable delay, they came back. So the meeting began.

The next day I wanted to go farther up the river. This was a side trip, actually, to explore the area; I had been told there were a couple of other villages farther on and I wanted to see for myself. I asked the chief if he could let me have a guide, since the area was new to me, and he called over a tall warrior and ordered him to go with me.

The guide was a powerful-looking man, naked from the waist up, with teeth that were filed down to sharp points. I did not know how well I was going to like him or how friendly he would be, and was happy to see that he was unarmed.

At any rate, we started up the river. It was a wild part of the world. There were no people, no houses, practically no signs whatever of civilization. This was the hot, green, humid backwoods into which these tribes had retreated before the advance of the white man, just as our own Indians in North America had fled back across the continent before the tide of exploration.

We had been traveling for about three hours when we saw a little hut standing in a clearing, back a short distance from the bank. It was rectangular shaped, with a thatched roof, a window, and a door. But what was extraordinary was its size; it was not much bigger than an overgrown doghouse, about four feet long, three feet wide, and no more than four or four and a half feet high.

"What do they keep in that house?" I asked our guide.

In broken Portuguese he answered, "That is where we keep our war birds."

"I would like to see them," I told him.

"No, you cannot. If you open the door they will get out."

"But if I open the door carefully so they do not get out?"

"If you open that door in time of peace," he said, "the old chief will cut off your head."

It isn't only women who are beset by curiosity. All day long I found myself tantalized by the desire to see what was in that birdhouse. On the way back, I devised a plan. As we came in front of the little clearing, I stopped the launch and told the Indian I could not go on without some oil. I needed only a small quantity, I said, but I had to have it. Well, I might have been able to go along without the extra supply he could get only down at the next village, but my guide fell for the story and shoved off in his canoe, which we had carried with us on the launch.

I waited until he had vanished around the first bend in the river. Then I hurried over to peek in the window of that house. Inside was a small bench built across the hut. On it stood two earthen jugs, about eight or ten inches high and six inches in diameter. On top of each jug was a dry banana leaf and on each leaf was a feathered bird— very dry and very dead. I went in and looked inside these jugs. I saw that there was a thick, brown substance in each. I learned later that this was curare, a poison brewed from the bark of trees and used on arrows. If a skirmish broke out between tribes, they could come by here and each man could dip his arrows in the earthen jugs of poison. That was why the guide did not want me to see what the birds guarded.

When he returned I was waiting for him and we went on down the river. It had not occurred to me, until we reached the village early that night, that he might have laid a trap for me.

As we came into the shore and let down the gangplank, a big Indian jumped down into the boat. "The chief wants to see the man's head in a box."

For one instant I thought that my investigation of the hut had been seen and this was the result. I stalled. "What do you mean—head in a box? What box?"

"That box right there," the big Indian said, pointing.

Jessie, standing beside me, thought he was talking about the kerosene cartons we carried with us. Her face suddenly grew pale. In English she said, "They want to cut off our heads and put them in these boxes because they know you looked at the war birds."

Her voice was calm, but I knew she was thoroughly alarmed—and upset at me.

I insisted then that the chief tell us himself what it was he wanted. The old man stalked regally onto the launch and pointed to the victrola. "I want to see the man in the box," he insisted.

Then I remembered—the tenor singing on the record. The chief actually thought there was a man's head in there and he wanted to see it.

It appeared his curiosity equaled my own, as our two ways of living crossed.

In any case, I took the victrola out and, as I played records for him that evening, I tried to explain the mechanism. He marveled at it and shook his head, and I think he was finally convinced that there really was no head inside.

The Maués are not what we call wild Indians. Actually, theirs is a rather high state of development, compared to that of the tribes we found to the south and in the far western areas. These others lived on an almost prehistoric level, often just a shade above the animals. But the Maués still had—and in large measure have not surrendered—many primitive rites and customs and attitudes. We sent a teacher into this area for a time but we had to replace him because he was cross-eyed. The Indians have little patience with this infirmity; they destroy all infants born with any such defect. It is their belief that people with crossed eyes give the evil eye to those they look on.

Most of these Indians speak their own dialect. Practically none spoke or understood a word of English when we first encountered them, and only a few knew Portuguese. I remember once, when we were vaccinating a number of them against smallpox, we saw two very ancient ladies standing by themselves. They must have been between ninety and a hundred years old. As we were finishing up, I said, "We have vaccinated everyone except those two young ladies in the corner."

The Indians who understood Portuguese began to laugh

and the two old women wanted to know what the joke was, so one of the men translated what I had said. One of the women said something in reply and all the Indians began to roar.

Then it was translated for me: "She says if she is a young girl, then she wants to be your daughter-in-law."

They were a people of humor and gentleness—and violence. Often they combine wisdom and cunning with a naïveté that is almost childlike. They had never seen ice before we arrived and the refrigerator on the *Luzeiro* was a source of wonder and delight to them. They also liked to rub their feet over the smooth, cool linoleum on the floor of our cabins. They enjoyed staying on the boat and often, if we had sick to care for, we would have to hurry them along. Jessie worked out a way of getting them out of the boat. She would take out a tray of ice cubes and put one in the hand of each Indian. They would change it from hand to hand as the cold penetrated. Finally, Jessie would say, "If you want to get that home before it melts, you had better go right now." They would all leave at once, and we would be left to go on with whatever we had to do.

Once the old chief called me to his hut to make a serious inquiry: What did I know about alarm clocks? It seems he had bought one when they had gone to the city, but it had gone only one day. Then it had stopped and had not run again in months. He had not realized that he had to wind it up when it ran down.

The morals of these people have always been very high. They do not practice polygamy and their home life is in most cases happy. The women do most of the work; the men do the hunting and fishing. But their marriage rituals are unique and extraordinary; the prospective bridegroom is put through one of the most terrible ordeals imaginable.

The beginning is like many other primitive courtships, however. If a man wishes to marry a girl in the tribe, he first must get the consent of her father. Once he obtains this, he goes to the girl's mother and gets her permission. He is then able to call on the young lady of his choice. Finally, the wedding arrangements are completed.

For the ceremony, the tribespeople make two large gloves, tightly woven of straw. They are decorated with the bright feathers of birds to make them as beautiful as possible. Next, nuts are gathered in the woods and strung, to be used later in the ceremony. They give out a hollow ring when jangled, almost like a string of bells. Finally, they collect an insect found in that region—it is known as the tocandeira. The savage and poisonous sting of these tiny wasplike insects with their glittering wings hurts almost unbearably for about twenty-four hours, and there is no known way—short of morphine—to deaden the pain.

However, the Indians have developed a vegetable compound which can anesthetize the insect itself. A dose of this over the nest of these insects puts them to sleep, but does not kill them. While these creatures are in their comatose state, about eighty of them are put in each of the gloves, with their wings delicately woven into the straw, so that the stingers face in toward the hand. On the wedding day, about an hour before the ceremony, the committee in charge of the festivities blows smoke into the gloves. The insects are awakened by this and, angered, they struggle to strike back.

At the given hour, the bride and bridegroom appear, and the "wedding bells"—the strings of nut shells gathered in the woods—are placed on the leg of the bridegroom at the knee. This is one instance where, if the wedding bells ring, there is no wedding. For the bridegroom must not shake or quiver while he goes through his ordeal.

Now the young man holds up his hands and, while his bride stands in front of him to watch, the gloves, with the angry insects inside, are placed on his hands.

As a hundred and sixty angry insects sting him, all at once, the bridegroom must stand there unmoving and unshaken. If his legs tremble or his body quails to a point where the bells on his knee sound, the young lady will refuse him. If he cries out, or grimaces, or complains, she will refuse to have him as her husband. This is the law.

Sometimes the man's arms swell up to twice their normal size after this ceremony. Sometimes the bridegroom dies. But if he withstands the test, and if he survives, he and the lady are considered from that moment on to be duly wed, and the gloves are hung upon the wall of their home as their wedding certificate.

No wonder polygamy is unknown among the Maués!

The primitive character of these Indians becomes just as apparent when trouble or danger strikes. I recall one occasion when some enterprising man had conceived the idea of building a rosewood distillery near one of the villages on the Andirá. This is one of the hundreds of varieties of hardwood found in the Amazon Valley; out of it is distilled a valuable rose-perfume extract. The large trees are chopped down and run through a machine that slices them up into little chips from which the perfume is extracted. The extract goes to America or France to be used in manufacturing commercial perfumes.

This man's plan in building a rosewood distillery near the village was that the Indians would get him the rosewood at low cost and work in his plant for a few cents a day. The Indians, however, did not like the idea of having their domain invaded by this man and his factory.

Their method of opposing his activity was direct. When I arrived in the village, hundreds of Indians from farther up the river had come to join in a war meeting. Five chiefs were present for this conclave, and about two thousand poisoned arrows were neatly stacked up and ready to go. Their plan was to make a direct attack on the factory and its operators, kill the owner and all the others involved, and burn the place down.

That, they said, would get rid of the rosewood operations forever, and discourage any other invaders with similar notions.

While hundreds of braves milled around ominously, the chiefs deliberated; and because they trusted me, they permitted me to listen and even to counsel them. I advised them to use moderation. "If you go off like this and destroy and kill, you will only bring down trouble and death upon yourselves. Why do you not try to resolve it peacefully?"

The chiefs looked at me grimly. "How? What way of peace, Senhor Leo?"

"The governor in Manaus. He is in charge of this district. Choose one of your chiefs to go to him and tell him that you do not want this rosewood plant on the outskirts of your village."

After further discussion, they decided that perhaps I was right. The poisoned arrows were put away and the Indian warriors sent home. A single chief was sent up to Manaus. He returned some days later with the joyful news that the governor was all on the side of the Indians.

Shortly thereafter, the rosewood plant was moved and

the war birds were undoubtedly replaced on the banana leaves which cover the urns of curare.

Civilization is a matter of comparison and definition. The lower tidal basin of the river is considered a comparatively civilized region, yet one does not have to go far from Belém to find dense jungles. We average, after all, over 80 inches of rain a year, all along the river. A little farther back from the stream, there is often more open forest with less of the thick undergrowth and many giant trees. Most of the land is flat and forested, and there are large areas in the western part—about fifteen hundred miles from Belém—where white men have never set foot. In some regions, back from the main river, we would come upon Indian villages, only to discover, on our return, no one and nothing. The nomadic Indians, following the game and the food, have moved on.

At certain times of year they stay near the long sandy beaches that line parts of the main river. The turtles, which sometimes weigh up to 150 pounds, come there to dig holes and lay eggs. The Indians come to live for a time off the turtle eggs and the turtles themselves. At other times of the year they go where there is more animal life, deer, wild hogs, buffalo; there are great herds of buffalo, direct descendants of animals brought over from Africa by the Portuguese. These beasts don't live in the jungles but in the more open places, especially on the island of Marajó at the mouth of the Amazon.

The wild boars, hunted both for their skins and their meat, travel in large herds. Once, going up the Amazon, we ran into fifty or seventy of them, swimming together across the river. Sometimes, if a hunter shoots one, the entire herd will turn and attack him, and to save his life he will have to climb a tree. I know of hunters who have been stranded all day in a tree, waiting for the angry animals to abandon the siege.

The river is a strange neighborhood of customs and ways unlike any other place on earth. In this labyrinth of riverways and jungle trails, over the years, we gathered a whole glittering notion counter of detail that is really a way of life.

I think, for instance, of a little stream upriver where once, long ago, a group of our directors and I anchored for the night. In the morning, one of them, a man named Ulrich Wissner, got up early and, when he saw how clear the water was, took out his dental plate to clean it. As he was doing this, the boat lurched and Ulrich's teeth disappeared into the depths.

"Well, there goes six hundred cruzeiros to the bottom of the river," he said resignedly.

From that time on, this stream became known all along the river as "The Place Where Wissner Lost His Teeth." Some time later, when this director came to the river again, this time with his wife, the thing she wanted most to see was this spot. When we showed her the place she looked long into the water and then said, with her quaint German accent, "Well, I suppose some alligator is using my husband's teeth now."

Often the losses on the river are far more disastrous. The floods sweep away livestock and farms and lives. The streams change and shift with the tides, and the rains and the flood waters swirl down from the Andes. At floodtime the river is a coiling monster, lashing out in its fury, spuming death and devastation in its uncontrolled rage.

Raising cattle is a major operation along the river, but many farmers have no high ground to which to take their animals during times of high water. Their solution is to build platforms and rafts of logs. Whole herds of cattle stand on these until the flood waters recede—often for several months—and the farmers have to go out and cut grass and bring it in their canoes to these animals to try to keep them alive. Many of the cattle don't survive. It is not unusual to see a raft crowded with other animals as well: hogs and chickens, even cats and other household pets.

It is at this time that many of the green-grass islands are pulled away from the banks and carried down the rivers; often they are several miles or more in length. Sometimes a farmer will "capture" a small grass island, tie a rope to it, and tug it, little by little, over to the platform where his livestock is standing. Then he will have feed close at hand.

During floodtime—it usually begins in the spring, which is the northern hemisphere's fall, and runs on into January and February—houses also are flooded along the riverbanks and for miles back. As the torrent begins to swirl through the house, the unlucky owners put logs down on the floor and a raised floor on top of the logs. If the water keeps rising, they put down another layer of logs and another floor eight or nine inches higher. They do this as long as they can, but if the water rises too swiftly, they have to abandon their houses to the flood and flee for their lives.

It is fantastic to see how fast the water can rise. One of our church members told me that one night, when her baby fell from his hammock, she had to rescue him from the waters sweeping in through the door to a depth of three feet.

The Amazon is a world of strange sights, strange moments, strange experiences. On a small stream that serves as a short cut into a larger river in the area of the Brevis Islands, we came around a bend to see a high tree on the bank. It had almost no leaves, but was covered with old clothes, pants, shirts, socks and pajamas, skirts, colored ribbons and tattered hats, all dangling grotesquely from its limbs.

We asked the friend who was guiding us through this short cut and he told us the legend of the old-clothes tree of the Amazon.

"Years and years ago a man was coming through this stream in a large canoe with four men rowing him while he sat in a reclining chair in the stern. Suddenly the canoe began to spin around in a circle. The water was deep but the canoe would not go on, either upstream or down. In despair they looked around and over on the riverbank they saw a mermaid sitting under the tree, naked.

"She asked them for clothes and the man opened his trunk, took out several articles of clothing, and threw them to her. The mermaid left and the canoe proceeded on its course. From that day on, everyone who goes by here in a canoe must put a piece of old clothing on the tree or, if they have no clothes to spare, must turn what they have inside out before they continue on their journey. The place is called 'The Bend Where You Turn Your Shirt.' "

So do stories and traditions start and live in the labyrinth that is the Amazon. Just below the modern city of Manaus in the Negro River is a beautiful little island, only about a mile long and five hundred feet wide. It is known as Conscience Island. When I asked about the name I was told, "Years ago when the rubber workers came here, seeking their fortunes, they checked their consciences on this island, and went on into the jungles. None ever stopped to reclaim his on the way back."

All along the Amazon there is wildlife in abundance: birds, ducks of every variety and plumage, fish of all types, alligators, and beasts of prey. In the early days alligators were plentiful everywhere, many of them twenty feet long or more. After being called on often to treat these creatures' victims, I didn't have to leave my conscience behind to strike back at these predators. Once a year we would hold an alligator hunt on the *Luzeiro*—usually for visiting directors from Rio or the States. I have shot many alligators at night, when it is easy to see them by the reflected light of their eyes, like two little electric lamps sitting motionless in the water. I remember one of our boat boys exclaiming one night, as an alligator lying in the water a few yards out from the boat closed his eyes, "Look—he turned out his light!"

The labyrinth also is a place of sounds, a thousand little half-heard sounds. Here is a man who asks us to lend him our shotgun; while we wait on the boat, he will go out in the woods and shoot us a deer. So we lend him our gun and some shells, and off he goes into the woods. A little later we hear shots and we begin thinking of venison steaks, but when he comes back he is dragging a big jaguar.

The man dumps this huge dead Amazon tiger before us and tells us what happened. As he had been going along the trail, looking for deer, he noticed the song of the cigarra, the locust of the Amazon. As he would pass a tree, the cigarra would stop its song for an instant as it always does in time of danger. Then it would start up again. An instant later, it would halt again, as if another peril was upon it. There must be, our hunter decided, someone or something following him.

He stepped into the shadow of the trees, turned, and looked back along the trail. There, outstalking his evening meal, was the jaguar. The hunter raised his gun and fired, before the animal could spring.

Such is this labyrinth of green in which we lived and worked. But it had its other side, too, in our personal lives, and in the sacrifices we had to make to carry on our work for these river people. We were parents as well as missionaries; our children were dear to us; and many times it was heartbreaking for us to have to leave them in Belém, while we went hundreds of miles away into the most inaccessible regions of the Amazon. Our wonderful workers cared for them, but still it was not like being with them ourselves. Always they would come down to the *Luzeiro* to say good-by, and always they would be waiting for us on our return.

As they grew older, the question of their education and their future became paramount. We knew at last that we would have to face up to the question which we had, in a way, been dodging, trying to put off the inevitable decision.

This is a question that each missionary must ask himself and to which only he can give the answer: In a life dedicated to the work of the Lord, how much does the missionary owe to the service of others, and how great is his obligation to his own?

Our life, Jessie's and mine, was adventurous and exciting. At least half of every year we were on the river, going from village to village, following some narrow winding stream along green corridors to a sick child or mother, to a community that needed us, to someone who wanted something. And never knowing, for certain, what lay beyond the next bend.

But it was a lonely life, too. Our children we could not take with us, except on that first trip. As Jack grew up, he went to school in Belém. Marian followed him a few years later. Each year, as we set out on our long journey, we found it harder to leave.

Once little Marian came down with whooping cough in Belém. A change of environment is sometimes recommended for this disease, so we took her with us for a couple of weeks on the boat. As soon as she was better she was up and in her bathing suit and diving off the side of the boat like some diminutive mermaid, enjoying the morning sun and the cool shade and clear water. "Don't worry," she would tell us, "I will watch out for alligators and big fish and nothing will hurt me."

And nothing ever did.

At another time, when we were coming back from a three-month trip into a very wild part of the river, we arrived at Maués to find a letter from Marian. The children were back in Belém under the care of Dona Maria, a Brazilian national and one of our reliable church workers, who was also a strict disciplinarian. One of her jobs was to keep little Marian from having too many cakes and cookies and other sweets.

Jessie tore open the envelope. "Dear Mother," Marian had written. "Please hurry home. Dona Maria won't give me any more butter."

Somehow that letter with its childish phrasing summed up much that was in our hearts, and Jessie didn't sleep very well that night as she pondered over our problem.

At that time Marian was living with Dona Maria and her husband, an Adventist pastor, in Belém. Jack, who was fifteen, was staying in our apartment to look after things, and taking his meals at the pastor's home. Once Dona Maria asked him if he wasn't afraid to stay all alone in the apartment. "Why, I'm not alone," Jack answered. "Jesus is with me, and also Fox, our police dog."

When Jack was ready for high school, we decided to let him go south to our school in São Paulo. It was a hard decision to make, for it meant that we would be with him even less; but Jack was a self-reliant youth, and we knew he would do well in his work in the advanced school. Then in 1936 came our furlough to the States and Jack came north to go back with us to the States. By this time he already had two years of college and he was full of school and studies and plans for his life. He wanted to go to college in America now, the Pacific Union College near Anguin, California. If we returned to Brazil, Jack would remain in our native land. While he had been away in São Paulo, in Brazil, many hundreds of miles to the south, still it was not as far distant as another continent, on the other side of the equator.

By that time Marian was thirteen, and we were deeply concerned about her education and future, too. We wanted her to have the advantages of an education in the States, with all that this would mean to her. We thought of other missionaries who had given up their work in the field because of the need to see their children through school at home. Now the question had come squarely to us, as we began preparations for our furlough. To leave our daughter in America, too, would mean a terrible separation. Then both our children would be away from us. Marian was still so young. Who was there to care for her in the States? This was the problem that worried us day and night at this time of our lives. Then one day Jessie said to me, "Doesn't David tell us to 'cast thy burden upon the Lord and he will sustain thee'? Isn't that how we should let this be resolved?"

That night we decided, Jessie and I, to make a proposition and ask the Lord to answer us by a certain sign. We had our obligations to these people of the Amazon; we had promised, by taking this assignment, to look after their needs, and certainly those needs were still great and our work was far from done. On the other hand, we had assumed the responsibility of caring for our daughter. Our parents in the States, on both sides, were too old to look after her. That she should have proper care was the heart of the problem. So we left it in the Lord's hands. And the sign we asked for was to be this: If, when we returned to Belém after a brief trip, there should be word from someone who would be able to care for our daughter in the States, and if this should come completely unsolicited, then it would be a sign from the Lord that we should leave Marian in America and return to the Amazon to complete our work.

We told no one of this but kept our own counsel and left on this trip which, we knew, might well be our last on the Amazon. But as we went from village to village, treating thousands of sick, hearing "Até o ano" from a hundred voices, we never said good-by but answered always, "Até o ano—si Deus quizer"—"Until next year if the Lord is willing."

We wondered, as we rounded Parrot Island on our way back into Belém, what was in store for us, and we had never before been so eager to look over our mail. A huge stack had piled up and, squarely on top, was a letter postmarked Washington, D.C. It proved to be from a friend of ours, a nurse. She was concerned about us and our work and our family; she'd been thinking of us, she wrote, and wondered if we had given any thought to Marian's future. Perhaps we would like to have her educated in the United States. If this were so, she said, she would be happy to take care of her for as long as we or she might wish.

We had asked for a sign and it had come to us, so directly and so powerfully, that it was almost stunning.

We would take our children back to America. And when our year's furlough was over we would return by ourselves to the labyrinth of the river.

CHAPTER 10

A TEACHER DIGS A GRAVE

BOTH Jessie and I knew that we had no right to think of ourselves as martyrs because of this separation from our children. Our son was on the West Coast in the States, Marian on the East Coast; both were in good hands and we did not have to worry about them. Far greater sacrifices than this temporary separation were being made by others because of the importance of education for all children, and adults as well. Even for those of this river to which Jessie and I returned, alone, to carry on our work.

In terms of sacrifice and devotion in the cause of education—of leading these people and their children out of the darkness of ignorance—Jessie and I always think of a teacher named Honorino Taveres, his lovely wife Maria, their dog and their chickens and their cow, and their infant son.

Honorino was a light-haired Brazilian who came from southern Brazil, where he had been a teacher for several years. Loyal members of our church, this teacher and his wife decided that their greatest service could come in bringing light into the green-shadowed world of the river. If they reached only a few, they made a start, Honorino said, in all his young enthusiasm. Like a pebble in the sea, the waves would spread out from wherever they began.

They had decided to start their work in a remote area on the Andirá River where the Indian tribes had had little contact with white people and none at all on any prolonged everyday basis. There was no school of any kind in this region; theirs was to be a pioneering effort, and we did not know what the reaction of the natives might be.

We took Honorino and his family to their destination in the *Luzeiro*. We had an extra canoe in tow, and the cow and chickens and dog, a few furnishings, luggage, and the family itself.

When we arrived—the trip took several days—we were greeted with the usual bowing and indications of welcome. But there was a noticeable reserve in the manner of the Indians; there were no smiles on their faces as they watched us unload. We told the chief why Honorino and his family had come; this was to be the teacher to help them and their children; we would build a school.

The chief nodded as if in understanding assent. But the others around him gave no such indication and from their expressions we sensed a wave of hostility. The night of our arrival, they put on a ritual to which we were not invited; we were told it was a devil dance. Almost all night we were kept awake by the loud and incessant pounding of the drums.

I was worried about what might happen, but the hostility did not break out into any open acts at that time. We talked with the chief and his advisers, the elder men of the tribe, and after a few days they agreed that it would be good to build a school for their children, and a house for the teacher. The chief called the Indians together to tell them of our plans and they agreed, also, saying they would help us put up the school and the teacher's home. The chief assigned Honorino and his family a house to live in until their place was finished. (It happened to be, we learned afterward, the home of the local witch doctor, who at that time was away in another village.)

With these arrangements made, we felt safe in leaving our teacher and his family in this far-off place, to live and work among these people. I will always remember the sight of that couple standing on the bank waving to us with their white handkerchiefs—and when we got farther away, with a white towel—as we drew away from the bank and headed down the river.

For a time all went smoothly. The chief had staked out a line, on one side of which was to be the village, on the other the school and the house for the teacher. We had drawn up plans and had laid out the positions for the two buildings. Work went along swiftly on the school; the frame was up and the roof was on by the time the witch doctor returned. But when he discovered what was going on, he was furious. These white strangers represented a threat to his own teachings and his authority and, to add insult to injury, they were living in his house!

They were ordered out at once and the only place for them to move into—all of them, including the baby—was the still half-finished schoolhouse, minus walls or any protection from the dampness and the tropical winds and rains.

The rainy season had just begun and the storms whipped through the half-finished building with such a rage that everything was drenched for days. The baby caught a cold which turned into pneumonia. The enmity of the witch doctor and his supporters continued. Our onetime guide, who was one of them, killed the teacher's dog and did everything he could to drive Honorino out.

A strange, grim war went on in this village between a man and woman fighting to save the life of their infant, and a village of Indians, half friendly, half hostile.

Honorino and Maria lost their battle to save their baby. The conditions under which they were forced to live were too much for the tiny son to combat, and after a few days of terrible fever he died. The two of them were alone in this rain-swept village of primitive terror.

Together they took counsel. Their first step, whatever else they did, whether they decided to go or stay, was to bury the baby. The Indians have their own rites of burial, but of these this missionary couple wanted no part. The father borrowed a spade, went out into a clearing, and began to dig, with his own hands, his son's grave. With his own hands, also, he nailed together rough-hewn pine timbers to make a tiny coffin.

The Indians watched in silence as all this went on, following each step of the way with wordless intensity. They themselves care little about the dead beyond the ritualistic stage; at any rate they do not appear to grieve deeply when a loved one is lost—their attitude seems to be that he is gone and that's that.

Yet there was something different about this and they were aware of it as Honorino ploddingly, step by step, did what he had to do. By himself, with Maria following, he carried the small coffin to the grave. The rain poured down with its endless symphony against the leaves as these sorrowing parents stood there while the father said a prayer and read a few words of Holy Scripture. "Lo, I am with you always," he read, "even unto the end of the world."

Silent, unsmiling still, the Indians looked on, standing a little distance away. They had killed Honorino's dog and cow, and stolen his chickens, and done all they could, largely under the instigation of our former guide, to drive these two out. Now they appeared somewhat touched by this ceremony.

As Honorino and Maria turned away, the chief approached them. "Will you still stay and teach? Or will you go down the river and join the white boat?"

"We are staying," Honorino answered. "If we were to run away, we would have brought on the death of our child for a worthless cause. We do not think it is worthless. Can you understand that?"

Slowly, the chief nodded. "It will not be without purpose, what you are doing here," he told them.

Subtly, in a way the young teacher could not explain, the attitude of the Indians changed. The building of the school and the house went forward swiftly; despite the witch doctor and his coterie of followers, most of the Indians began working hard to complete them.

After long weeks the school and the house were finished. Some of the Indians began to attend services held by the teacher on the Sabbath. They began to send their youngsters to school. Teaching and training and holding meetings in the midst of a people many of whom had been enemies, this bereaved father and mother forgot their loss and their sorrow. Maria taught the Indian women to knit and cook. As a result of the school and the dedication of this man and woman, the lives of these primitive people changed completely.

There was a postscript to this story that was especially heart-warming to us.

Once, long after Honorino and Maria began their work, we held a meeting of these Indians, who, under the gentle influence of these two wonderful people, had become friendly.

Afterward, our onetime guide asked if he could go with us down the river. I knew him only from that one trip; I did not know the role he had played in trying to drive out our teacher.

It was about eleven o'clock when we left the village, and overhead the skies were stormy and dark. As I sat steering the *Luzeiro* through the night, my thoughts eddied around the grim story of the teacher who had first come here, his courage in the face of the Indians' opposition, and his victory.

I was brought back to earth by our Indian hitchhiker, who had crowded so close to me that he was almost pushing me off my seat. As I wondered what his nudging meant, suddenly he whispered to me, "I wish to ask a favor. Could you have your wife sing again the song she sang at the meeting tonight?"

I called Jessie, and she came forward and sang the hymn called "Christ Saves Sinners." Jessie has a pleasing voice and it was lovely to hear her there in the night. When she finished, the Indian asked her to sing it all over again.

Finally, when she had gone through it a second time, the Indian asked, "Did Jesus die to save all sinners everywhere —or only the white man?"

"Why, He died to save all of us," Jessie said.

"I am a very wicked man," the Indian said gravely. "I tried to kill the teacher and I did kill his dog and had his cow destroyed and stole his chickens. I have killed six men in my life—six men." He paused. "Do you think He could forgive me *my* sins?"

"Jesus is our Saviour," I said. "He is ready to forgive any who come to Him with repentance in their hearts, regardless of who they are or what they have done in the past."

"I want to know Him," this Indian said, his voice so low we could scarcely hear.

Education is regarded in our faith as vital to the training for a Christian life. This is why, wherever we go with our missions, we build schools and hospitals and clinics as well as churches. Our goal is to build up mind, body, and soul—to educate "the mind, heart, and hand"—and through this threefold effort to make the individual capable of sound judgments of his own. We teach; we do not indoctrinate. We train but we do not regiment. We guide but do not seek to compel.

In many places along the Amazon, youngsters had no opportunity at all for education, and the starting of schools has always been one of our purposes in the area, as far as our limited funds would permit. By 1958, when Jessie and I returned to America, our church was operating some twenty schools in the Amazon Valley, with more than a thousand youngsters enrolled. The schools are of different types. The first one we set up, in the neighborhood of the Maués Indians, was what we call a mission school, where adults as well as children are taught. Other schools are primarily for children. In all of them the problem is threefold—spiritual, academic, and manual. Pupils must work at least two hours a day, to help defray part of the expenses of their own education and to train them for work.

The first Adventist school in Brazil goes back half a

century in São Paulo, where a few classes were started in a one-room schoolhouse built with what little money was available. Located just outside São Paulo in Santo Amaro, today it has become a magnificent college, with a total of about seven hundred students in residence each year. Its principal object is to prepare them for the ministry, but in addition to theological courses it gives commercial- and normal-school training as well. It is fully accredited by the Brazilian government.

Our school program along the Amazon was not so ambitious. It developed as our missionary activity progressed, and it advanced in a variety of ways, sometimes where we recognized a need and took the lead in starting a school, sometimes where the natives provided the impetus. As word spread of our schools and our teachers—missionaries or church members usually—we began to get many requests. Unfortunately we had neither the funds nor the personnel, trained or even partially trained, to send to all the school-less communities which asked for them.

Once, I recall, three Indians arrived in Fortaleza, capital of the state of Ceará. This is a modern city on the Atlantic Ocean, with a population of more than a hundred thousand; and the sight of three Indians, barefoot and in native dress, with their long hair flowing down to their shoulders, attracted as much attention as they would have on Chicago's Michigan Boulevard. But the natives were oblivious to the stares. They had just one thing in mind: to find the people who operated the boats on the Amazon River and had opened schools for children. At last they located our minister in charge of the Fortaleza Mission, Pastor Roger Wilcox.

The oldest of the three was their spokesman: "Our chief

sent us to find these people. I am the chief's brother; these are his sons. We need help. We are here to get a teacher for our tribe."

"You came a long way?" Wilcox asked.

"Yes," the older man said. "We have walked this entire way. It has taken us thirty-one days and each day we walked many kilometers."

Pastor Wilcox looked down at their bare feet, which had brought them over jungles and dusty roads to this city by the sea.

"As soon as we can find a teacher who can go, we will send him to you," he promised them.

Happy with this promise, the three started their long trek home. But finding a teacher and the funds to finance a school was easier said than done. Months later, the three Indians returned. "The old chief is old and gray and his eyes grow dim," they told the pastor. "Each morning we carry him to the river to see the teacher, but none has come."

Again, with only a promise that they would get a teacher as soon as possible, the three men had to start home.

One day a teacher will go there. But at that time we had no funds to hire one, nor any man or woman prepared to go.

Classes in most of our schools along the river extend from the first through the fifth grade, as do the Brazilian public schools. Above that are junior high and high school. Most of our work was with the primary grades, but we have an academy in the state of Pernambuco, where, for higher education, we send students from as far off as Manaus, 750 miles away. In Belém itself, on the river, another academy was under construction when we left Brazil.

Our schools are accepted by the state authorities in Brazil and maintain the highest standards. Our teachers are either graduates of our own institutions or of the state normal schools. Funds to run them are obtained in several ways, but come primarily from church allocations and—where they can afford it—from the families of the pupils.

In Belém, all but one of our seven churches also maintain their own school. In most Brazilian schools, classes run only half a day; but in certain of our schools we hold two sessions, our teachers taking one group in the morning and another in the afternoon. Along the river, particularly, in addition to the three R's, we give courses in planting and cultivating the ground, and in cleanliness and body hygiene, and in all schools we have Bible classes for spiritual instruction. Our schools are open to persons of all faiths; religious instruction is based on the Bible and its prophecies.

Each of our schools operates on an annual budget. From 30 to 40 per cent of a teacher's salary is paid by the mission, which also furnishes the building and equipment required. Remaining funds come from tuition and from the church organization. Where parents can't afford to pay, the church makes up the difference.

The schools along the river were primitive; some of them reminded me of my early teaching days in the Rockies, when the youngsters used to stack their guns outside the door before coming in for class. And, like those rural schools in the States, they were used for other purposes, too.

I arranged to hold a meeting one night in one of our early schools, built on a knoll high above the river. It was to be for both the grownups and the children of our group, and all the youngsters were getting themselves spruced up for the occasion. I was there early, looking on while one of our members was acting as barber, cutting a youngster's hair. The little fellow was perched on the desk where the teacher sat during classes—and from which I would preach in the evening—when I noticed something moving under the table. I called some of our group and, as we snatched the boy to safety, we found a bushmaster snake on a ledge under the table top. They dispatched the snake with their big knives, and the meeting was postponed until they found the other—bushmasters always travel in pairs —and destroyed it.

But snakes and wild animals and floods and the difficulties of transportation—none of these could halt our school program for long. In Belém, in Manaus, in the little towns along the Amazon, wherever some few people came together to form a church group, there followed quickly a school for their children. Literally thousands of youngsters have learned the rudiments of education in these schools built in the jungles—children who in other years would have been illiterates all their lives. And many of these children have gone on to our college in São Paulo, or to schools and colleges in other cities, following their elementary education in one of these "little palm schoolhouses" on the river. Many have taught others, in their own tribes, in the backwashes beyond where we or our teachers reached. Knowledge spreads like seeds on the wind, carried from one town to the next, from one individual to another.

One story I like in connection with our schools involves one of our colporteurs who sold Bibles and religious literature along the river and a blind man on whom he called. This book salesman had been told that this blind man wouldn't buy any Bibles or books; after all, he couldn't even see. But the colporteur had an impulsion to talk with him, without necessarily trying to sell him anything at all. He didn't even tell the blind man at first what he did, only that he was engaged in Gospel work and had stopped in to visit and comfort him.

So they talked of religion, the colporteur said a brief prayer, and then rose to go. As he reached the door, the blind man said, "Now, what is your real business? I know that you have not come all this distance simply to comfort me and say a prayer. You must have some business or something to sell."

The colporteur smiled. After a moment he said, "You are right. I am selling books about religion, and I am selling the Bible; but because you could not see to read any of that, I did not try to sell you anything."

The man was interested in the Bible. Could he hear some of it? The salesman took out a copy and turned to a passage with which he was familiar, in Isaiah (28:18): "And in that day shall the deaf hear the words of the book, and the eyes of the blind shall see. . . ."

The blind man listened attentively as the colporteur read. "Let me feel the book," he said then. "Let me hold it in my hand."

The colporteur handed it to him, and the man carefully felt the covers and ran his fingers over the smooth pages. He asked how much it cost. The price was eighty cruzeiros, the salesman told him. "Go open the big trunk," the man called out to his wife in the next room, "and bring me the money."

"I can't read or write," the woman said, as she appeared.

But the sale was completed, and the blind man, holding the Bible, told her: "Now go get a new towel, wrap up this book carefully, and put it in the trunk."

The colporteur was curious. What did they plan to do with the Book, he asked. "There is a school near here," the man told him. "It has been started by your people, I seem to remember. I have a grandson who is now of school age, and I am going to talk with this teacher today and see if she will take in my grandson, so that he will learn to read and someday he will be able to read this Book to me."

Our schools, and the broad educational program which operates throughout Brazil as in all countries where our missionaries are active, are more than merely an arm of the church; they are an endeavor to bring new light and meaning to the lives of the people. To Jessie and me, the school that symbolizes most what this work means lies in an area due south of Belém. It is in this region that one reaches the mouth of the River of Death. As this is written, no white man has ever gone up this stream and returned alive.

It was in this general area that Theodore Roosevelt made his expedition up the River of Doubt, now called the River of Roosevelt. All of this country is jungle, much of it unexplored. The forests conceal hostile tribes whose arrows rain down on any invaders.

To reach this part of the world and establish a school was a hazardous operation for us, even after our many years on the riverways of the Amazon, but in the middle 1950's we set out. It was to be our last major pioneering activity before our return to America.

The main "highway" into this area is the Tocantins

River, the last great tributary to enter the Amazon before it spills into the Atlantic. About fifty miles wide at the point where it joins the Amazon, this huge stream follows a generally southerly course through jungles and forests wilder than any we had seen before. Some distance south we came to another large river, the Araguaia, along whose banks are the Chevantes Indians. They were really savage, we had been warned, and had always been hostile to all white men. Every night, as we proceeded on our way, we stopped on the east side of the stream; had we ventured to the west bank, we would have been showered with poisoned arrows.

Chugging upstream, we came to the Island of Bananas and, shortly beyond, the Rio Morte (The River of Death) and the River of Doubt. Here, on the island and the east shore of the Araguaia, there is another tribe, the Carajas. It was with them that we hoped to start our work in this region.

They were supposed to have become more docile than the Chevantes, and less given to aiming poisoned arrows at strangers, but they were still in a wild state, wore practically no clothing, and their way of life was extremely primitive. The men, who were husky enough to do the heaviest sort of work, were hunters and fishermen only. What planting was done—a few cassava roots and some fruits—was taken care of by the women.

As they lived close to the water, they were all on hand to watch as the *Luzeiro* pulled in to shore and we disembarked with our gifts—several hundred fish hooks of various sizes, a quantity of fish line, combs, looking glasses, small knives, and (because we had been told that they went around naked most of the time) five sacks of used clothing. We distributed the presents and the clothing, and had them dress up for us; but before I could even get motion pictures of them in their new apparel, they ran back to their huts, took off their clothes, carefully put them away, and came back as naked as ever.

Only a few years before, this tribe had been hostile and ready to kill any white man who came into their area. Now, even though they would not wear our clothes (except at night to keep warm), they welcomed us as friends, taking us with them on a fishing trip, guiding us through parts of the woods where they hunted, and showing us the places where they did their planting. They even put on one of their ceremonial dances and permitted us to make motion pictures. On that occasion the men dressed in grass clothing with grotesque masks over their faces and huge and often magnificent headgear. The women, however, wore even less than usual.

There was savage excitement in their pagan ceremonial. Yet these Indians seemed to be reaching out for something beyond this level of development. The gnarled, powerfully built chief talked to us about this, begging us to send them a teacher so they could learn to read and write and to speak Portuguese and also begin to learn a better way of life. He was quite in earnest about it.

On our return to the Mission Office in Goiós, we made an appeal to our superior organization in the south and were granted extra funds with which to organize a school for the Carajas. Within a year from our visit, we sent a man-and-wife team into this district to take on the job. We have a nice school building there; the wife teaches and the man shows the Indians how to plant, use machinery, and till their soil more efficiently.

To help us with this program with the "wild Indians," the Brazilian government has given them some farm equipment, a grist mill, a motor, and a small portable electric plant and lights. The schoolhouse is busy morning and night; the youngsters study during the day, and the "adult education" program of the three R's is carried on in the evening. It is a real transformation.

Shortly after the school was opened, the old chief of the savage Chevantes tribe died. He left two sons and, as happens even in civilized areas, the two had a bitter quarrel as to which should be head now. The quarrel ended in a split of the tribe into two groups. The wilder ones elected to go even farther up the Rio Morte, deeper into the shadows they appeared anxious to draw around themselves. The younger brother drew around him the more tractable members of the tribe.

The younger son and his followers moved to a place on the west bank of the Araguaia, not far from the Island of Bananas where our school is located. By this time, reports had begun to circulate about what was going on among the Carajas, with the white man's help. Finally, the young chief of the Chevantes sent over a delegation of twenty-four warriors. After they had put on a dance and made every effort to be friendly, they wanted to know: Could they have a teacher for their tribe also?

We proceeded with the utmost caution with these people, as they had in the past killed many white folk. However, we are aware that a new regime has come into existence under the younger brother's leadership and we are hoping to send them a teacher and begin the educational and spiritual work they call for—at last—on the River of Death.

The tides of custom change, like the currents of the river.

On the Isle of Bananas, among the Carajas Indians, there is a curious puberty ritual for the young men. In the center of the village is the *banco de honra*—the bench of honor—to which, one at a time, each boy of the proper adolescent age must come. When he sits on this bench it means that he has arrived at a point where he is leaving boyhood and turning to manhood. But there must be an outward sign of his courage and fortitude.

For this, the witch doctor has prepared a little bone only a few inches long, taken out of the shank of a deer. With this he pierces a hole through the youth's lower lip, from the inside out. He then treats it with a charcoal preparation so that it does not become infected. When this heals, it leaves a small hole through which the young man can pass the deer bone. Inside is attached a cross-piece, made of another bone, about three-quarters of an inch in length, to keep the longer bone from falling out.

So the young Indian now has his symbol of manhood. Often, in giving a direction, the Indians use the bone in their mouth to point the way, in a bizarre, grotesque gesture.

One day, less than a year after our school there opened, one of the boys who had gone through this puberty ritual came to our teacher and said, in broken Portuguese, "I have reached a decision. I am finished with this." He drew the thin, sharp-pointed piece of deer bone out of his mouth and put it on the desk. "I will never wear this again."

His whole appearance and expression changed with that bizarre bit of pagan decoration gone. His lips broke into a wide boyish grin. "I am not any more a savage," he said, with great pride.

CHAPTER 11

A TREE OF TEARS

THE witch doctor is outlawed in most Brazilian cities, yet he continues to carry on his activities and to flourish in many of them. In remote areas his power increases, usually in direct ratio to the distance from civilization, science, and true religion. In the regions least touched by the modern world, he becomes a dictator, whose herbs and brews, incantations and decisions and punishments, are accepted by all as the inevitable judgment before which they must bow; his prescription is the only safeguard against demons on the loose; his muttered word is the law for all to accept and obey; in his dark foreboding nod is life or death.

He plays on the fears and the ignorance of his tribe or village with consummate skill. He is doctor and judge and priest, jury and executioner, and in each role he claims special powers and authority. In areas where there is no doctor, he is usually the only person to whom the people can turn in time of sickness. If his brew fails, then it was the devil's fault. If it succeeds, it was the witch doctor's skill. In one case I heard about, a witch doctor prescribed as a medicine a tea brewed from an old pipe that had been broken up into a hundred pieces. The nicotine in the pipe was so strong that it killed the patient, but the witch doctor blamed the evil spirits for having killed the man in spite of the "medicine."

Certainly the life-and-death drama of a little girl named Yvonne is an episode one can scarcely imagine happening in our mid-twentieth century, in a region over which fly some of our great airliners, only hours out of New York's International Airport, en route to Rio or Buenos Aires.

Among the wilder Indians to the west—out in the never-never world that lies on the borders between Brazil and Peru—are the Campos Indians. These tribes live in the largely unexplored region around the Javari River, an extension of the Solimões. Among them the witch doctor is almost a living god. Whatever happens in the tribe is his province to examine; if there is a death, it is up to him to decide by his rituals who is responsible; that individual, whoever he may be, must be punished.

There are only four major punishments among these Indians. First, they tie a rock around the guilty one's foot and throw him into the middle of the river. Second, they tie him to a tree or a stake and leave him for wild animals to tear apart and eat. Third, they tie him to a tree and build a slow fire around it, so he will burn to death. The fourth punishment is to break his skin, put honey all over him, and tie him down over an anthill, so that these insects will strip away his flesh.

Not many years ago, when one of the leading warriors came to an untimely end, the witch doctor prepared his brews to determine who was guilty. In his large pot he put all kinds of items: alligator meat, snake meat, toads, frogs, herbs. When his brew was boiling, the witch doctor inhaled its steam, breathing deeply and rhythmically, and

then announced that the spirits in this compound had re-
vealed to him the one who caused this tragic death.

It was Yvonne, a lovely child of nine, the darling of all,
the cherub. Her mother screamed and drew the little girl
to her, crying out that Yvonne had done nothing, that her
spirit knowingly or unknowingly could not have willed
the warrior dead.

The medicine man was unmoved. She was guilty, he
repeated; the spirits do not lie about such things. She
must be tied to a tree and a slow fire built around her.
There she will be kept until she is consumed in the flames
for causing in her evil thoughts the death of this man.

The decision was made in the late afternoon. The
execution was set for dawn the next day.

As night came, the mother tried to think of some way of
escape. No one was supposed to protest the orders of the
witch doctor, no matter how grim the punishment he
meted out, and therefore neither the child nor the mother
was locked up. After all, where could they run? To the
certain death of the jungle on all sides? To the alligators
on the riverbanks?

They could not hold back the dawn. Yet only seven
hours away, down the river, was an Adventist mission
station. The mother had heard of it and of the American
who ran it, Pastor S. A. Rusker. If they could reach this
mission, the mother thought, they would be safe. The
witch doctor would not have any authority there, and
therefore could not claim the girl's life.

Just before midnight, the mother and Yvonne slipped
out of their hut and down to the river's edge. In the darkness they got into the smallest canoe they could find and
started out down the stream. They paddled all night long

through the dark, aware that when the witch doctor found they had fled he would be in a fury.

When daybreak came the witch doctor arose, put on his ceremonial garments, and went to get his little victim, only to find that she and her mother were gone. His rage and frustration erupted in a great roar that echoed across the woods. The cry went up: "The girl must be brought back!" Otherwise, the death of the warrior, which the spirits say she caused by her evil thoughts, would remain unpunished. The medicine man called twenty warriors who agreed to set out at once to find her. It didn't take them long to discover that a canoe was missing; they knew then that mother and child could only have fled down-river.

Twenty men in a canoe can paddle much faster than one woman and a child, and even a head start is not tremendous against such odds. As they rounded each curve and bend, the Indians expected to see their quarry just ahead, but to their surprise the mother and daughter were not in sight.

But they were gaining steadily on this pair in flight before them. Both the mother and girl paddled with all their strength. As dawn broke, the exhausted pair were just half a mile from the mission. But behind them they could see the large canoe with the twenty warriors and the witch doctor bearing down on them. Their head start of time had almost run out. But in spite of their terror they kept on. The mother headed the canoe swiftly into the riverbank, they leapt out and ran along the shore and up a little hill toward the mission.

Friendly Indians, most of them Christians, came out to greet them. Exhausted, sobbing in sheer panic, mother and daughter collapsed into the arms of these men and were carried by them into the mission just as the pursuing Campos beached their big canoe and came running up the hill after them.

Inside the mission, the friendly Indians turned the mother and Yvonne over to Pastor Rusker's protection.

The warriors and their witch doctor surrounded the mission and began to bellow out demands for the pair, threatening to burn down the building if they were not turned over at once. Rusker came to the door to tell the savages they could not have this mother and child to murder.

The witch doctor shouted back that they would go and get all their tribe and return and destroy the mission people and the Indians who supported them. As the medicine man poured out his stream of venomous imprecations, Pastor Rusker stood in the doorway, unarmed and unconcerned for his own safety. They would not get Yvonne or her mother, he said firmly. If they tried to take either by force, he would not be responsible for what the friendly Indians of the mission would do to them.

The warriors were suddenly aware that they were outnumbered, and that the pastor was not quailing before them or their witch doctor. Avenging the death of one of their own began to seem less important than staying alive themselves. The witch doctor tried to make a show of it. "Come, we will go back for a council of war," he announced loudly, as the twenty braves climbed into their canoe and started back to their people—in complete defeat.

I talked with one of the young lady workers at that mission a few years ago. I had heard the story of the little girl and her mother from several people who had been there and I was anxious to meet the girl herself. The young lady said, "Yvonne? I am Yvonne, but I am not a little girl now. You know, it was a few years ago—that terrible night."

It was from her that I got all the details of that story.

One of the most dangerous things about the witch doctors is that they are trusted so completely by these simple people who, so often, have nothing more substantial in which to believe. And the more the witch doctor dresses up his humbug in obscure ritual with overtones of terror, the more certain he is of holding them in his power.

In one far-off place, a seven-year-old child became ill simply because of lack of hygienic living. Her little body was covered with sores; she was so anemic that she was little more than a living skeleton. The mother was ignorant and without funds. She loved her daughter, but she decided that her best course was to give the little girl to someone who could afford to give her medical care. In return, the child would grow up to be a servant for these people. It would be better, her mother thought, for the girl to be an indentured servant for the rest of her life than to be free—but dead.

So the mother took her skeleton of a child down the river to her new home and left her there, satisfied that this family would give the child medical care.

As soon as the mother had gone, the family with whom this pitiful little girl had been left called in the witch doctor, a half-breed Indian, who went through a mumbo-jumbo of incantations and finally was "possessed" of the spirits which told him the "cure" for the child's illness.

On the bank of the river, to the left of the house, was a filthy pen where a few hogs wallowed. The witch doctor ordered the family to keep the child in this pigsty for three days with very little food or water, but with a medicine he would give her that would drive out the evil spirits which had possession of her. These spirits, he explained, would go into the hogs and the little girl would then be well.

The head of the family was a little concerned lest the spirits might destroy his hogs, but the witch doctor assured him that there was no danger, that evil spirits like these could live in hogs indefinitely without harming them.

So, on the orders of this witch doctor, the half-dead little girl was put almost naked into the hogpen and left there. That same day, on a river boat which put into the village to take on shipments of rubber and Brazil nuts, was a woman passenger. Strolling around the town, she saw the child in the hogpen and at once demanded to know what was going on. The villagers explained that it was the witch doctor's orders. None dared disobey, the child must be left there alone for three days.

But the visitor was unimpressed and insisted that the child be released at once. Before anyone could stop her, she snatched up the little girl and carried her on board just seconds before the river steamer lifted anchor and pulled away. In her cabin she gave the child a bath, got her some clothes, and asked the boat's nurse to give the child a penicillin shot and treat the sores on her little body.

As they went on downstream, the woman began to wonder what to do with the poor child she had rescued. She was getting all kinds of advice from everyone on board, when someone happened to see the *Luzeiro III,* with Walter Streithorst at the wheel. The river boat stopped and its captain called to Walter: "We have a little girl here who needs special care. Can you take her?"

"Of course, we'll take her," came the answer.

In midstream the seven-year-old was transferred to the *Luzeiro*, where she was treated with all the love and care Walter and Olga could give her. When the launch reached Manaus, its home port, she was given additional medical treatment and, with proper diet and hygiene, began to put on weight and blossom out. A kindly woman in Manaus took the girl and has given her a wonderful home, is sending her to school, and today this lovely child scarcely remembers the terrible time when she was so close to death in the hogpen.

To our faces, the witch doctors were always our friends, making big talk about favoring our work and praising what we were doing. But behind our backs, they continually denounced us and in a hundred ways tried to undermine us and our efforts. At the same time, they helped to keep alive and to spread superstitions of many kinds. This was not difficult, certainly, in the aura of ignorance and fear and legend which permeated so many parts of the river.

There is, for example, a certain fish from which three small bones are taken. The uneducated river folk believe that, if sewed into a little bag and worn around the neck, these bones will keep away any sickness. Therefore they will pay almost any price to obtain them.

They are also great believers in the efficacy of an alligator's tooth to ward off bad luck. To keep them safe from snakebite, they bore a tiny hole in the tooth and wear it on a cord around the ankle. Many people—of all classes, including the well-educated and some church-going Christians—have this superstition so ingrained that they would not dream of going into a field or forest without an alligator's tooth. This belief is much stronger and taken far more seriously than, for example, the American custom of carrying a rabbit's foot for good luck.

I spent an evening once with a man who believed so much in the power of the alligator's tooth that he had one tied around the neck of each of his cows, and assured me that this was the reason none of them had been bitten by snakes. When I tried to find out why he was so firmly convinced, he told me a story about a time when he and a friend were building a house. Every evening they would light a fire to cook their supper and regularly a bushmaster snake—the variety that is attracted to fires—would appear and with its writhing body extinguish the flame.

"We had a nice house cat with us," the alligator-tooth advocate said, "and my friend and I decided to try an experiment. We weren't afraid of this snake and we wanted to see what would happen. So one night I took off the alligator's tooth which I was wearing around my ankle and put it around the cat's neck. When the bushmaster appeared, we threw the cat right down on top of it. The cat bristled up and the snake bristled back and then turned and slipped out into the woods.

"The next night the snake was back again, and again we had the tooth around the cat and threw it down on the bushmaster. Once more the snake slipped away into the woods without harming the cat.

"The night after that, we took the alligator's tooth off the cat before throwing him down on the snake and this time the bushmaster instantly struck the animal and killed him.

"So, you see, we have proof."

I tried to point out that his "proof" appeared to be little more than coincidence, or possibly merely an example of an even-tempered bushmaster which would put up with just so much trouble from a cat. But I got nowhere with my argument.

Many people try to make real commercial operations out of superstitions. I remember a typical operator who "kept shop" right in the city of Manaus, on a raft down by the water front. There, among the crowded wharves with their ever-present smell of fish, he sat day after day, with all his dolls and figurines and bottles and potions spread out like the merchandise on a drugstore counter.

In this big, modern city he carried on a lively trade with medicines and mixtures that would cure any disease. He had a preparation that would, he claimed, grow hair on bald heads—but it wasn't quite ready to show. He had figurines that were guaranteed to help in all kinds of problems. He had a soap that wouldn't make any lather. (I bought a cake of it and discovered that it wouldn't clean either.)

He was, however, a talkative and friendly merchant and reminded me somewhat of the medicine-show men who sometimes turned up in our Nebraska towns half a century ago.

Once he asked Jessie and me to translate a letter he had received from a company in New York City. The firm might be interested, it said, in doing business with him. It gave the company's bank reference, and asked him for *his* bank reference as a preliminary step.

When Jessie told him all this, he said, "Bank? Here's my bank right here," and made a gesture in the direction of his raft, with his bottles and idols and all the rest. "If they don't want to do business with me on my terms, they don't have to."

And they didn't.

Another interesting personality along the river was not a witch doctor but a snake doctor, who claimed to possess medicines and powers that would cure any snakebite. No one appeared to know exactly what he did or how, but he used a variety of medicines and herbs and was reported to have a good deal of success in effecting cures.

In Óbidos, where he lived, and elsewhere along the river, the stories of his feats were legion. Why, we were told, he will let a snake bite a dog and the dog will die within seconds. Then he will let the snake bite him and he will be unharmed.

One of his medicines, he claimed, would "protect" the user from snakebite for several weeks at a time. To many who used it, the medicine appeared to work, and consequently he made a great deal of money out of it. His reputation became such that the scientists at the snake farm at Butantan—the world's center for the production of anti-snakebite serum—invited him to come down and give a full-scale demonstration. They were not convinced of his claims or of the authenticity of his snakebite protection.

Our snake doctor went down to the Butantan Institute in São Paulo, apparently full of confidence, but somehow, in front of all those learned scientists who had devoted their lives to this subject, his magic arts failed utterly. He allowed himself to be bitten and promptly became so ill from the effects of the bite that all the science and skill of the Institute had to be called into operation to save his life.

The man returned to his home on the river, greatly disappointed at his showing at Butantan, but full of excuses: the change of climate, the atmosphere of doubt and hostility, and all the rest. Many people believed him and continued to give him their support. When last I heard, he was training his son to take over his business after he retired.

One superstition widely accepted in the river world and through most of northern Brazil is that of *mau olhado* —the "bad eye" or "evil eye." There are people who claim to have this power so fully developed that they can put a jinx on anyone just by looking him once in the eye. I heard of one woman who was supposed to be able to look at a fruit tree in such a way that it would never bear again. Once I saw a withered tree in a yard in Belém. "What's wrong with that mango tree?" I asked the owners.

"The woman came and looked at it with the bad eye," I was told.

I said it could not be true. "You don't believe," they said, as though I should be ashamed.

"No, I do not believe that story," I told them. "And I never will."

We found this "bad eye" superstition all along the Amazon. If a person was sick, then someone must have looked at him with the evil eye. A mother is afraid to let you hold her baby lest you harm the infant by looking at it with the bad eye.

There are rituals for getting people to fall in love and for making them fall out of love, for putting together a marriage—or trying to break one up.

A woman trying to win a reluctant male will go to the witch doctor, who mixes together coarse corn meal, a certain red oil made from a tree, and the blood from the head of a freshly killed rooster. After a ceremony in the street, including incantations and "hand passes" over this mixture, the man may as well give up. Reluctant or not, he's hooked.

Sometimes there is great fear that *feitiço*—witchcraft—is being used to break up a home. Jessie and I were staying once at the home of a cultured lady, the wife of a doctor. In the morning, immediately after the man had left for his office, his wife jumped up from the breakfast table and hurried to the window. Her father-in-law, who was eating with us, asked her what she was looking at.

"That woman across the street has started witchcraft against my husband to take him from me," the wife said. "I wanted to see what she was doing."

Devil worship of various types is also practiced, not openly in the big cities, but often only a few miles away, on the outskirts. This is the sort of thing we think of in America as "voodoo," and often results in susceptible people's going into trances that may last hours or even days. People go out from the city to watch and laugh, but the effects are not always funny.

Once, at church in Belém, when one of our important pastors was preaching, I was seated next to a youngish woman and her son. As the service went on, the woman began to rock back and forth in a strange manner. After this had continued for some time, the little boy said, "Mother, please, let's go."

"What is wrong with her—is she sick?" I asked.

The child shook his head. *"Bicho de fundo"*—"It is a spirit from the evil world."

The woman kept on rocking, apparently in a trance, until finally she toppled over. I got up and called a policeman, and he and I together half carried, half dragged her out through the crowded church. We were scarcely outside when she went into a kind of trancelike spasm and pulled all her clothes up over her head. If ever anyone needed help, she did—and she got it. Medical care and some psychotherapy improved her condition greatly.

Along the river world, the superstitious also have strange ideas about the moon and its effects. Many feel that their lives are completely controlled by this globe in the heavens. If they want to go to town, they must go when the moon is in exactly the right position. A tree for lumber must be cut in the dark of the moon; otherwise, the wood burrs will hatch out and eat up the wood. Crops planted when the moon is wrong will never ripen. Some things are started when the moon is new, some when it is at the full. There is a pattern of good and bad in these things, and only the witch doctor can be sure.

Burial beliefs and rituals vary widely from tribe to tribe. Some of the most interesting are found among the Carajas on the Island of Bananas, along the Rio Araguaia. These people bury their dead in shallow graves for six months, with their bows and arrows and war clubs at their sides. Each day during that period they carry food and drink to the departed ones, to help them find their way into the spirit world. But after six months it is assumed that the spirits have left their earthly forms and need them no longer, for they have rotted away. Then the Indians remove the bodies, clean off the flesh, and place the bones in urns. In a Caraja cemetery what we saw were these earthenware urns piled up, one on top of the other, six or eight or ten high, an entire family together. Wherever we looked there were the stacked-up urns of the dead.

It was among these same Indians that we found the custom of the weeping tree. This is actually a piqui, which, at a certain time of year, bears a lovely yellow flower. Among the Carajas there is a law that when anyone dies the tribespeople must weep and carry on until the flowers fall off the tree. This is not too bad if the death occurs a few days before the flowers fall, but if it is weeks or months earlier, the mourning becomes a terrific burden. Someone must be at the tree all the time, day and night, and the sound of the moaning and weeping was so terrible when we were there that we would pull our boat out of range for a little while each afternoon to get away from the sound of weeping.

I was told that when some of the very old or decrepit become ill at about the time the leaves are going to fall, the others do all they can to hurry them on their way, even to the point of withholding nourishment, so that they will die before the yellow blossoms fall.

CHAPTER 12

ARICATU!

THE true wilderness—the no man's land of the savages, the head-hunters, the wildest and most dangerous tribes, and those with the lowest cultural level—lies in the vast crescent bulge beyond Manaus, fed by the Negro, the Solimões, the Purus, and the Rio Branco, reaching north into the territory of Rio Branco, across the state of Amazonas and south into the territory of Guaporé. This is the true frontier world. It is the land of the head-hunters. Actual cannibalism I have not encountered, although it may exist; but head-hunting is a thriving business that still continues in this inaccessible and unworldly region "beyond the beyond."

The greater part of our work was carried on along the main streams of the Amazon between Belém and Manaus. There were comparatively civilized areas; the people could be reached with our help and teaching; and we felt that this was the best place to start. It was only later— around 1940—that we moved into the world beyond Manaus.

The country that fans out in all directions from this lovely city with its magnificent modern airport is one of the most untamed regions on earth. Perhaps the most striking example of its violence and bloodshed and terror is contained in the story of two men who tried to run away from the Word of God.

Pastor Storch had been holding a series of meetings in Manaus. Among the many hundreds who had been attending were a man who owned a big island in the river near Manaus, and his son-in-law. Apparently, in spite of themselves, something kept forcing them to come again and again. Finally, the older man said to the younger, "These speakers seem to be talking straight at us. If they keep on, we'll surrender and become converted, and I haven't any desire for that religious stuff. I suggest that we get out of the city now." Although he spoke half-jokingly, he was very much in earnest.

The younger man agreed and suggested a hunting party up the Negro River or one of its tributaries. "There are alligators up there by the thousands and these days they bring many cruzeiros a skin," he added.

These two invited ten other men, making a party of twelve, and got together everything they would need for a journey into the wilds—canoes, axes, guns, ammunition. Some miles up the black waters of the Negro, at the mouth of a tributary river, they encountered a man in a canoe who assured them that he knew this tributary well and that it was rich with alligators waiting to be killed. They took this man—the thirteenth—into their party.

They paddled all day through seemingly untouched wonder and beauty until they came, in the late afternoon, to a lovely *praia* or sandy beach. Here they decided to stop for the night.

It was an isolated, eerie world to which they had come. At that time of year wildlife was abundant and along the river were large fishing birds—white herons—as well as parrots and parakeets. Pulling their canoe up onto the beach, they began, in the midst of this wilderness, to pitch their camp for the night. But the older man and one other in the group felt they were taking too great a risk. "All of us are in the same basket," they told the others. "We are going to go down-river a ways. If anything happens to you, we may be able to get out. And if anything happens to us, you may have a chance to escape. It is much safer that way."

The two started on downstream to pitch their camp some miles below, leaving the others encamped on the *praia*.

About six-thirty the following morning, two large canoes of Indians appeared on the river and edged into the beach as the eleven men were rising.

One, evidently the Indians' leader, asked in bad Portuguese, "Where is your chief?"

They tried to tell him that the chief was farther down the river.

"I want to talk to the one in command," the leader insisted.

They again tried to explain that their leader was not there.

The chief then turned to the others and said just one word, "*Aricatu.*"

His men, standing behind him in a semicircle, lifted their bows and arrows, and shot. In a matter of seconds, as the arrows filled the quiet dawn, ten of the men lay sprawled in death on the silver strand of beach, stained now with their blood.

Only two of the party were not hit: the son-in-law and

a man who was too ill even to attempt to run. As the son-in-law tried to help the sick one to his feet, an arrow struck him, passing through his body. The son-in-law pulled it out and threw it to the ground without breaking it.

The Indian raced forward and picked up the arrow as the son-in-law ran on despite his terrible wound. The sick man did not have the strength to go on. As he fell back the Indian picked up the arrow and inserted it in the bow. His victim lifted his hands in a last effort to save his life, pleading to be spared in the name of Jesus, but the Indian had no knowledge of what that meant. He shot again—and killed.

Then the Indians turned and followed the son-in-law, who was bleeding from both front and back and was afraid to get into the water for fear the blood would attract the piranha, which would tear him to bits in seconds. But better the uncertainty of the fish than sure death from the Indians. He slid into the stream and swam as far as he could. No piranha, he thought gratefully, as he got out of the water. He looked cautiously about, saw only one Indian was following him. As the savage raised his bow, the wounded man dived back into the river and swam under water a little way, in spite of his loss of blood. The shot missed and, since no others followed, he decided the savage had used his last arrow.

The son-in-law headed for the woods. Holding one hand on his back to catch the blood from his gaping wound, he would smear it on his chest to keep it from leaving a trail. Near complete collapse from exhaustion, he climbed a tree, and settled back in a notch to rest. But rest was not to come. In the branches was a nest of ants about three quarters of an inch long. Attracted to the blood, they nearly ate him up.

All was quiet in the sunlit woods. Any moment this tortured, bleeding man expected to see the Indians come out of the jungle. None came. The quiet bothered him. Then he heard a noise. Or was it only his mind? He was the only one who had escaped. If anyone was approaching, it was an enemy. He heard the sound again, footsteps drawing nearer. In an instant he expected to see an arrow fly out of that dense foliage. Then he heard a voice, words being spoken, repeated. *"Vale me Deus,"* he heard: "God protect me."

As he saw the man emerge from the trees, he recognized him as one of the eleven who had been attacked. He was also wounded, but his wound was in the shoulder and not serious. They hid until nightfall and then, under cover, made their way back to the river. All was silent there; the Indians were gone. So, too, were the canoes. The two men hid near the shore until dawn. Then they started down the stream on a raft they put together with logs and vines.

It was hardly heavy enough for their weight and they sank into the water up to their chests. But they started. Both had developed fever and the water seemed to keep it down. All day they floated along on the raft, wounded and feverish and fighting mosquitoes and flies. All through the next night they kept on, always aware that the Indians might return to finish their work.

The following morning, as it grew light, they saw a launch approaching. In it were the two men who had made camp farther downstream. Seeing the Indians, they had decided the best thing they could do was to go for help. Near the point where the river joins the Negro, they had run into a motor launch; on this boat were Brazilian nationals who agreed to search for the other eleven, despite the risk involved for all on board. There was medicine on board, and the two injured men were bathed and bandaged and fed while the boat chugged on upriver to the beach that had seemed so peaceful and lovely when they had decided to camp there for the night. The sight that met them was, for sheer barbarity, almost beyond belief. The Indians had taken their victims' axes, machetes, and big knives, intended for alligator killing, and had literally chopped them to pieces!

In silence, the men on the launch dug a grave on the beach and, with a prayer of commitment to God, the nine victims of the attack were buried.

On their return to Manaus, the older man and his son-in-law were treated at a hospital. When they were fully recovered the younger man told the father-in-law, "I think we should join this church from which we tried to run. This was the start of all that terrible tragedy on the river."

The other agreed and both have become important members—the younger man is in charge of all missionary activity in this church. Few men could have such reason to know the meaning of this work.

Our own efforts "beyond the beyond" began in 1940, when we made our first journey west of Manaus, first on the Solimões, which for some distance above Manaus is more heavily populated than below. It is a rich, fertile region of bananas, oranges, and rubber. Up on the Purus River, about six days from Manaus, a group was waiting for us. We found a house for a meeting but, the first night, toads were attracted by the light and made such a racket that we could scarcely be heard.

The next night one of the men came up to me and said, "Do you have a flashlight? If you do, I'll play policeman to those toads." I got him a flashlight and he got himself a club. He stood outside with his weapons while I preached. Every now and then I would see his light flash and hear a loud thudding sound. But we heard no toads. When our service was over, our toad policeman announced, "There're twenty-eight of 'em lying outside that won't ever again try to break up a prayer meeting."

When we got away from the populated areas, there was a desolate quality to this part of the river. The people, living in widely separated villages and areas along its banks, are different from those farther downstream. For one reason or another, they were frightened of us. They ran when we approached; hid when we entered a village. Some are Indians, some are of mixed blood, a few are nationals. The most important one, of whatever blood, is the man who runs the store, who sells the others their food and their Brazilian brand of whisky. In almost any direction from the villages along the main rivers are the areas of the wildest Indians. The Indians here are far different from those in other lands, including North America. The latter had to be industrious to stay alive and feed their families; to keep warm in winter; to store up food. None of that is true of these tribes. For them it is summer all year round. They have a constant supply of food, and there is no need for them to protect themselves against the elements. Hence they live from day to day.

In the northern regions of this interior world, most of the Brazilian Indians use the blowgun. A primitive weapon to begin with, it has been perfected by them and its use is a highly developed art. It is made, very accurately, out of a long, hard, narrow piece of wood and to this writing no one knows how these unschooled folk accurately cut this strip in two, hollow out each half, and glue the two pieces back together almost perfectly. However they accomplish this, they then, with sand and a string, rub the inside until it is silky smooth. This harmless-looking gadget is used to fire poison-tipped darts eight to ten inches long, and by a technique involving a piece of string wound around the end of the dart to hold in the air, an expert apparently can build up air pressure so that he can "shoot" his dart thirty to forty yards with accuracy.

These Indians, whose level of culture is higher than those to the south, have developed curare solutions in varying strength. With some they kill; with others they only knock out their victim. This enables them to capture live monkeys easily—for sale or for pets.

To the south are some of the most primitive tribes still in existence. With one group, the Pacanovos, we have not been able to make direct contact at all. One missionary who had been there for some time told me he took them many presents in order to win their friendship, and was able to travel with them for a while. One of them died because he had no resistance to the germs of the white man and caught a cold that developed into pneumonia.

The dead man was not buried. His widow put his body on her back and the whole tribe moved out of the area of death. The missionary went with them. After several days of travel, they stopped, cut up the corpse, dug a hole, and cremated the body. Then they wrapped the ashes in a banana leaf and the woman carried them off with her.

The Pacanovos have no houses, this missionary reported, and no fixed residences. When the rainy season comes, they put poles against a tree, lay a few banana or palm leaves over the top, and live under their improvised shelter. When they are hungry they eat whatever fruit is available, or kill an animal. Often they eat the meat raw, with their hands, simply tearing the flesh apart, almost like animals.

But as far as I know, the most savage Indians are the Jibaros. They are a large tribe and are divided into many branches, but all of them seem to have the same basic instinct—they are cold-blooded killers. Some live in Brazil, some in Peru. The boundaries in that area are not always clearly marked.

Usually called *caçadors de cabeça*—hunters of the heads —they are truly a murderous people, and with their faces tattooed into grotesque masks of terror and their fantastic headgear, decorated with feathers of the large tucan bird, they look as savage as they are.

To them, murder is a way of life, a ritual and ceremony, and an act of honor. Of late years, since shrunken heads became something of a big business, they have had an additional incentive for killing. They will lie in ambush for hours, waiting for an enemy or a prospective victim— male or female—to pass. Then they attack, first with their blowguns, and then with their bone spears.

The heads are cut off immediately and shrunk, I understand, by a technique involving hot stones and water and the breaking of the bones. This, at least, was the report of De Graaf, a great explorer and the only white man, I believe, who ever saw heads actually in the process of being shrunk. The finished product is called by the Indians *shanas*.

One grotesque story is told of a German who went down to Peru not many years ago on one of the big liners. When he left the boat at Callao, port city of Lima, he told the captain, "When you get here a few trips from now, in about two months, I will go back with you."

The captain had forgotten all about his former passenger when he came into port two months later and took on board another explorer, who was heading back north. Among the trophies he proudly displayed was a shrunken head he had bought for five dollars.

According to the story, the captain gave a cry of horror as he recognized the German passenger who had assured him he would go back on this very trip.

One sight we saw in this area was the railroad that cost, as the saying there goes, "a life for every tie." Begun by the French in 1900, taken over by the English, and ultimately finished by Americans, who had most of the ties shipped in from Australia, this road bypassed the falls and rapids of the Mamore River, which forms the boundary between Bolivia and Brazil, and the Madeira River. About 225 miles long, it is called the Mamore-Madeira Railroad.

The Indians in the area are still wild and dangerous. They did everything they could to prevent the laying of this track, even to shooting poisoned arrows at workers who were already plagued by malaria and other diseases that cost hundreds of lives. American engineers strung high-tension wires around the construction groups—and the murder rate fell sharply.

As I looked at this railroad, I found myself thinking of the tracks the Union Pacific had stretched across the great state of Nebraska, in North America, and of the Sioux Indians there who made their raids across the river Platte, threatened my grandparents with fire and death, and tried to lasso locomotives and pull them from the tracks.

CHAPTER 13

INTO ALL THE WORLD

IN one of the towns along the river, a group was preparing for baptism in the Christian church under our guidance. It included a number of young adults and one very old man. He had been twenty-three, he told me, at the time of a war in Paraguay; checking in the history books, we found he must now be in his hundredth year. He had studied the Bible and our Bible lessons and was well prepared. The problem was that the place of baptism was to be at a point twenty miles out of the city and the only way to get there was to walk. The old man—Emidio—told me not to worry. "I will be there, Senhor Leo."

The day of the long walk dawned hot and sunny. Emidio was not in our group as we set out. Several times we had to stop and rest and quench our thirst by eating oranges—the water we found along the way was not good. When we reached the baptismal place, Emidio was there waiting for us. The ninety-nine-year-old man had left at midnight the previous night to reach the place on time.

After the ceremony, all of the newly baptized, including Emidio, went with me to a rented hall, where we began to discuss plans for a church. We tried to get each person to give whatever he would in whatever way he could, time, energy, money, planning, materials. I saw that

Emidio had his hand raised high. I asked him what he could do to help with our building.

The old man arose and came forward so that all could see and hear. "I have cut timbers for three chapels in my life," the old man said, "and now if the Lord will give me the strength I will go out into the woods and cut timbers for this church to which I belong."

Despite the warnings of many of us that it was too much for him, the old man insisted. Each day he went into the forest, cut the wood for the beams, and helped to bring it out. Every beam needed for the church the old man hewed himself. It was not a chore for him, but a crusade. He did not live to see the actual opening of the church, but he did get to see his beams erected and the building take form and substance against the Amazon skies.

Emidio's joy in helping to build a place of worship is an example of its meaning in the lives of thousands of people with whom we worked. Their church was not a building to them but the center of their faith. In one community, not far from Belém, a group of lay preachers built a church big enough to hold more than a hundred and twenty worshipers. It was a solidly constructed building which took more than a year to build, and every bit of it was done by these men in addition to their regular work.

One church we built in 1954, at a place about eight hours below Manaus, is a floating church, as far as I know the only such in the world. Because of the sixty-foot rise in the river from October to June, and the resulting floods, it is difficult or impossible in some areas to find ground high enough for a church so that it can be used whether the water is high or low.

Our answer was a floating church. Built over three large

cedar trunks, each about six feet in diameter, it will hold more than two hundred worshipers. Around the edges we left room for a platform so the people can come to church in their canoes, tie them up to this floating side-walk, and, without even rumpling their Sabbath clothes, stroll into the building.

Our building program was—and is—a continuing ad-venture. We have constructed scores of churches of all types, shapes, and sizes along the Amazon, in Belém, and, in fact, throughout Brazil.

When a place of worship was needed quickly in San-tarém, about six hundred miles up the Amazon, one of our officials designed it, had most of the windows and door frames and other "prefabricated" sections made in Belém, put the material on a boat, and hauled it up the river. Seventeen days after its arrival, we had a church in actual use.

In 1954, we built a church at Macapá, on the northern bank of the Amazon near the mouth of the river. The equator passes through the middle of town—and through the middle of the church. When the minister stands up to to give his sermon, he is in the northern hemisphere; his congregation in the southern.

When Jessie and I arrived in Belém we had no church building. The room below our apartment was used for our meetings at first and later we hired a large theater. For it we paid what seemed like a large sum—but it was only about $4.00 a month in present terms. We distributed handbills announcing our services, and I would make my own slides for the projector by copying pictures onto glass slides and tinting them with water colors. I also used verses out of the Portuguese Bible, projected on cellophane paper.

That was how we started. Almost anyone who was interested would receive a visit from us. Gradually we built up our membership, and by 1935 our congregation had grown to such proportions that we had to build a real church. I had begun plans for it in 1932, and when we finally had the land and the funds, I took charge of the construction myself, to save expenses. It is a very beautiful modern church which holds three hundred people. Later, other buildings were added on this same property, including an office building and residence and two schools. As our congregation in Belém grew, other churches were put up, and by 1958, when Jessie and I left for America, Belém had seven beautiful churches for our more than one thousand four hundred members there.

Before our arrival, the Amazon people had been in the habit of coming to the city once a year for a festival period, partly religious, partly merely to have a time of celebration. Many of them did not want to give up this custom, so we decided that once a year we would hold a general meeting, bring all our people together, and have someone from the States or Rio speak to them and lead discussions. These have become camp meetings, very much like those in the States. Our plan was to present well-rounded programs that would cover a great many areas of importance. Not only did we hold services, but also classes in hygiene, child care, and home-building, with special emphasis on toilets and sanitation. Jessie gave the talks on hygiene and child care, and sometimes added classes in cooking. From time to time we would also have dialogues, panel groups, and practical demonstrations.

These "old-fashioned camp meetings" became, in fact, true conferences and seminars in the art of Christian living for native peoples and Indians.

How is a church begun along the river? In any of a hundred ways. Once, as we were chugging along upstream, we saw a man on the bank waving frantically for us to stop. He took us back into the woods about a mile to his village where a number of people had brought their sick to be treated. The village had no church, but the people wanted a meeting that night. However, they were so far back from the river that our power lines from the electric plant on the boat would not reach them and they had no electricity themselves. One of the men suggested that they could cut a clearing in the jungle along the bank and hold the meeting there. Every able-bodied man in the village, it seemed to me, got out his ax and hurried down to the water's edge. Soon the stream echoed and re-echoed to the sound of their axes and the crashing down of trees. By nightfall they had cleared out a rectangular space where I set up my projector, tacked up a sheet between two trees for a screen, and we were ready to begin.

By seven-thirty the place was crowded with men, women, and children. Another missionary, Pastor Steinweg, and his wife, who were with us, played a portable organ and we taught the group to sing hymns. Then I showed my slides and gave my lecture. There was a last hymn and the meeting was supposed to be over. But the people wanted more. Pastor Steinweg went out to the boat and got more slides, and we had another lecture and sang more hymns. When he was done, they wanted still more and I had to talk again. It was almost midnight when the meeting broke up.

Now, in that clearing, there is a church and a school-house; the woods all around have been cleared away; and there are many houses there—a flourishing little village has sprung up where there had been only jungle.

Once, when we were making a trip during floodtime on the river with the treasurer of our South American division and his wife, Mr. and Mrs. Owen Blake—he is now assistant treasurer at our world headquarters—we came to the house of one of our members who pleaded with us to hold a meeting that night. I said we would if he would send out and invite his neighbors. He agreed, adding that the neighbors lived a little distance away.

At eight o'clock that evening, I had my projector and screen set up and ready to go. Walter Streithorst, who was going to do the preaching, was ready, too. The trouble was, not a soul had shown up. "Well, let's have the meeting anyway," Walter said, "just for this family." So we showed beautiful pictures, had a sermon, and sang some hymns. All just for the family and ourselves.

About ten o'clock we turned out the lights on the boat and I was almost asleep when I heard a distant noise. It sounded like an engine. I looked down the river and saw a good-sized launch coming in our direction. As it drew closer I could see that it was jammed with people. "We hope we're not too late for the meeting," they called out. By that time it was getting close to eleven o'clock and both Walter and I were truly tired. But after a little grumbling from both of us, I heard myself saying, "Walter, these people apparently have come a long way; they have made a great effort to get here; we ought to make an effort to hold that meeting."

So we got up and I set up my projector all over again, and my screen. Exactly thirty-seven people trooped in from that boat for the meeting. The member at whose home we had stopped was particularly grateful; he had sent his launch all around the district to pick up these people and bring them to the meeting and he didn't want them disappointed.

Of course, the church building is more than just a structure. Its deepest meaning must be expressed in deeds, and the individual effort is often most dramatic. One of our members, now retired, developed a program of winning friends and converts to the Christian faith with white grape-juice bottles.

This man took the empty bottles, put a bit of religious literature in each, corked and sealed them with wax, and threw them into the Amazon. As the white bottles bobbed along with the current, people could see that something was inside. Since many of these people feel that whatever comes down the river into their hands is sent by fate itself, they read and considered seriously the message inside the bottles.

For a long time this unique propagandist for the church sent more than a hundred bottles a month down the Amazon, and at least a dozen people came into the Christian faith as a result, to our knowledge.

Where once we had only a handful of members and churches, today we have hundreds throughout the Amazon, and Brazil, and South America. In the state of São Paulo alone, for example, we have twenty-four churches.

Each of these churches—and the smaller chapels as

well—grows out of the need, the demand, of the people.

Along the river we stop at a home. Here is an eighteen-year-old girl who has leprosy. She becomes interested in the Bible. At last the progress of her illness reaches a point where she must be sent to a leper colony below Manaus. In the midst of this institution with its suffering people, in all stages of illness, this young woman carries on the work of Christ. She reads from the Bible and discusses its meaning. Soon she has formed a group within the leper colony.

Before very long these people are able, with help from our church organization, to build a chapel. Within five years, their membership has grown to fifty.

In 1942, in Santarém, I baptized a young man who was suffering from leprosy. It already covered his entire body and I felt sure it would not be long before he was sent to the colony. He was, however, a devout Bible student and his faith was very strong. As he came out of the water after his baptism, he told me, "One day I am going to be a minister and a worker in the Lord's cause."

After his baptism, he was separated from the rest of his family, keeping to one room where there was a door that had been cut in half so that the upper half would open. On the lower half was a ledge he could use as an altar. Because his family was not rich, church members took up a collection to put in electric light for him.

He liked to play the guitar and sing hymns, and he knew the Bible well. His mother would go out and bring in the neighbors, who would stand in the hall a little distance from the door. While he played the guitar, they would sing and study the Bible together. From this room, he converted twenty-three persons.

At the same time, we began giving him injections of some of the modern "miracle" compounds. They seemed to help him so we continued, supplying the drugs and teaching his family how to administer them. In all, he had more than 660 injections over a period of seven years. Toward the last we were using a Brazilian-made medicine called Promin.

Gradually he began to get better. He was so well, in fact, that his family began to take him to hospitals and clinics for blood tests and other examinations. Finally, he was able to obtain twenty-three certificates from doctors and medical institutions stating that there was no longer any trace of leprosy discoverable in his system.

He was taken on as an employee by our organization and did remarkable work for many years in the state of Piauí.

CHAPTER 14

RIVER PATTERNS

THE patterns of the river forever change and are forever the same. They are the patterns of ever-flowing excitement, of low water and flood. Homes along the water are usually built on stilts, but the hungry stream reaches up into them. There is constant struggle and conflict and swirling assault. The Amazon is so wide and so deep that we must carry a hundred feet of chain, merely to be able to anchor close in to the bank. The pattern of its floor has been mapped, and looking at these subterranean outlines one sees a world of valleys and mountains and rocks and weird patterns of growing, underwater forests—a sunken world of unguessed wonders.

The life we led on board our boat was far more than a day-to-day or hour-to-hour program of meals or treatments or meetings. Ours was the routine of the unexpected. We would be up at dawn, have our breakfast, and begin our day. We might be heading to Santarém or Manaus for supplies, but a canoe comes alongside, a white towel is waving in front of a house. All over the river "the white medical boat of the missionaries" is recognized. We are needed up there in that house, where someone is dying. A child is sick —its parents do not know what is wrong. Supplies must wait; we always stop where there is need.

I remember one passenger on the *Luzeiro* became impatient at all our stops. We were on our way to a meeting in which he was to participate and all that day people, in an area where malaria had broken out, were hailing us, asking us to treat them. How could we fail to answer their waving towels? But our visitor kept saying that, if we continued to stop, we would not make the meeting.

Seven days later, as this same man was heading south on the high seas, he came down with malaria himself and was so ill that he turned over his money and personal belongings to the ship's captain and wrote a farewell letter to his wife. The ship's doctor pulled him through. That his illness had taught him a little of the real meaning of our work came in a letter I received from him: "Brother Halliwell, in your work there, never pass a home where a poor soul is suffering with malaria. It doesn't matter how many sermons you preach, but never neglect someone with a terrible, terrible disease."

It was an injunction we had always followed—and always would.

We did not know and could not guess the pattern of our lives for even a single day. Here we reach a village where we have friends. They run to greet us, to invite us to meals, and to ask when we are holding a meeting. In the store, which is the heart of the town, people gather around to ask us questions about the city and the world outside, and they tell us their own news. A boy has been struck by an electric eel, stunned and drowned. The eel has since been killed. A woman whose husband had been desperately ill with malaria comes to tell us about him. We had given her a quantity of half-gram quinine pills and told her to give them to him three times a day for three days.

"Did you give him the medicine as we directed?" I ask.

The woman answers: "I gave it to him all at once. All nine pills at once."

Such a colossal dose ought to have killed him, but his wife tells us, "Oh, no. His ears rang and he was almost blind for a while—but now he's completely all right and the malaria is gone."

We hear the stories of families and individuals. Here are three girls, daughters of one of the leading farmers in this area. We helped to bring two of them into the world, years back. They were educated in the school we built in the district. Now grown, they are going down-river to study for a life in the business world and in nursing.

Outside, we meet a youngster we treated a few weeks back for snakebite. He is brimming over with health—and gratefulness. We remember when we first saw him, sitting there after our meeting was over.

"I have been bitten by a snake," he had said. "Can you help me?"

"Why did you sit there all this time?" I had demanded. "Delays can be very dangerous in these cases."

"Oh, I couldn't interrupt a religious meeting," this boy had said.

Now, fortunately, he is well.

We have lunch on the boat and invite in one or two of our friends. Jessie prepares a special meal of fish and fried bananas. There are many different kinds of bananas in Brazil and they are all wonderful—bananas are the perfect food, in fact—but the plantains are the ones I like best. They grow about fourteen or fifteen inches long. Jessie slices them lengthwise into long strips and fries them.

Then with a dash of sugar and cinnamon sprinkled on them, they make a wonderful tropical meal.

We move on in the afternoon toward a place a little farther along where some people are waiting for us to hold a meeting. We are stopped several times by the towels. In every home, it seems, someone is ill. We do not reach the place of the meeting we had scheduled until three days later.

On our arrival we find difficulties. There is a show troupe traveling through this area, putting on vaudeville. It is scheduled to use the only hall in the town tonight. The mayor asks us if we can hold our meeting out of doors. We agree. We drop over with the town official to ask the man who runs the show if he would mind starting his performance a little later than usual, to permit us to hold our meeting first.

He is somewhat aloof. Just what kind of meeting would I be holding? he asks. When I tell him it is a religious gathering he shrugs. "Hold it whenever you want. No religious meeting can take anybody away from my show," he tells us.

So we go ahead with our outdoor meeting. There is one building in the center of town with great white walls and I decide to use that as my screen. I get a box to hold the projector, and shortly after dark I begin to show beautiful color slides I had taken and had made up of Rio de Janeiro. When the gathered youngsters see these pictures they plead with me to wait until they can get their families. Four times I try to begin and each time I have to stop and wait. By eight o'clock it seems that every person in town is crowded around that building.

I doubt if we ever have had a more enthusiastic gathering. There are shouts and applause when the film is over. I announce then that I am going to preach for half an hour and that then I will show more pictures until ten o'clock. No one leaves. I talk about Bible prophecies, and then I go into a discussion of the evils of various vices, particularly gambling and drinking. A drunk tries to break up our meeting by asking if alcohol isn't good for snakebite, and everyone starts to laugh but the mayor has the man arrested. Another drunk interferes and the mayor ships him off to jail, too.

The owner of the show comes in to complain that he had not known we were going to show pictures or provide anything interesting.

"You had your chance," the mayor states. "You didn't think these missionaries had anything exciting to say, but now you know they do."

The showman continues to protest and only subsides when the mayor threatens to lock him up with the others.

It is the unexpected which is normal, in the town or under way. We ride through a school of fish in the moonlight, and thirty-seven leap into the boat. A friend from the States is at the table in the salon when a fish leaps through the open window and lands flapping and ready for frying—on the guest's dinner plate.

In Itocoatiana we find some cookies in a bakery which a guest of ours considers delicious. While he is munching one, a canoe goes by our boat with a load of alligator eggs. Our visitor says, "Ask him what he does with these eggs." The canoeist explains, "If I can't sell these eggs along the river, I take them in to the baker in Manaus. He uses them to make cookies."

Some of our guests on board the *Luzeiro* are fearful of the strange Amazon world. They note every unusual sound and often ask us, "Is something wrong? I heard the oddest noise." Usually it is nothing more than the wind, or some bird or animal or perhaps a leaping fish. They often get upset at the sounds of the motor; if the throb changes suddenly, they are sure disaster is close. A guest on one trip had received as a gift two parakeets and a parrot to take home to his sons in Rio. We had the birds in a crate in the engine room. Early in the morning this guest was awakened by a strange noise that he thought was coming out of the motor. "Something has gone wrong," he calls. "The engine is out of order."

It does indeed sound strange, and I get up and go aft to investigate. When I get to the engine room, our "peril" is cleared up. The three birds in their cages have entered into a running competition with the motor and are making the most incredible noises I have ever heard, trying to drown it out.

We laugh, our boat boy at the wheel laughs, and the *Luzeiro* rides on.

There are patterns, too, for the people who live along the river, for their customs and ways and habits.

Here is a couple we will call Jose and Maria. These two, like many along the river, are nationals; they were married a good many years before in a civil court. They have five boys and a girl, and live in a house at the water's edge. The walls might have been made of mud and clay; they are, in fact, made of woven palm leaves.

Both had been born and reared here in the Amazon Valley. The man grows coca and raises cattle and catches fish. The variety of fish along the river is infinite, but the simplest to catch are the piranha. Dangerous man-eating fish, if they get at you when you are in the water, they are so greedy for meat that they will take any bait that has meat on it and therefore they can be caught by the hundreds. Another fish often caught is the tambaque, which grows to twenty pounds or more and will eat only rubber seeds, Brazil nuts, or nuts out of the woods which fall from the plants and float down the streams.

We can bait our line with a nut or a bit of fruit, leave it set overnight, and in the morning find we have hooked a tambaque. Because of their odd diet, these fish are common in the waters of the woods when the river is over its banks. Fishermen set their lines then with fifty hooks or more—each baited with a nut—and often catch ten or even twenty fish at a time.

Once I saw a man in a canoe loaded with a couple of hundred of these beautiful tambaques and asked how he managed to catch so many. His answer was that he had learned to mimic the monkeys. "The monkeys go to a certain fruit tree and chatter a lot and spill fruit in the water, so the tambaques have learned to follow this noise. I imitate the monkeys, drop a little fruit into the water, and pretty soon I can pull in the fish as fast as I can bait the hooks."

Jose goes after the pirarucú, or red fish, which is taken usually with a harpoon. It has scales so hard they can be used for sandpaper, and its tongue sometimes serves as a nutmeg grater. Some Americans have dubbed the pirarucú the Amazon cod.

Jose has found of recent years that the fish in the river are not so plentiful as before, and the Brazilian government is beginning to make rules to protect fish life. The electric eels—chiefly the one called the *puraque*—are still found, but not in great numbers in the more populated areas. These eels can generate six hundred volts with a frequency of about six cycles a minute. Their voltage is high but there is no amperage; however, by placing an electrode over the positive pole and another over the negative pole, back near the tail, scientists have succeeded in ringing a doorbell and lighting a neon lamp by eel power alone.

Fish is one of the staple foods of the valley. In most houses the smell is ever present, and almost always there are fish hanging out on a line in the back. Each day the old are eaten or thrown away, and the newly caught hung up to dry, like clothes on a back-yard line.

The roof of Jose's house, like the others along the river, is covered with palm leaves. These will last, with minor repairs, for four or five years; then new palm-leaf "shingles" must be brought in. The house is thirty-five or forty feet long, divided inside into one main room and several sleeping rooms. The kitchen is a separate small house because Jose's wife, like the other women, cooks over an open wood fire. The kitchen is always large because it serves many purposes. Here Maria makes her manioc flour, with which she bakes a substitute for bread. The flour is made by draining out the poisonous water from the manioc root, drying it, and then heating it. The process produces a high-starch flour which is widely used in Brazil. Here also in the kitchen is stored a pile of unthreshed rice which is stomped out in a large black bowl on the floor as it is needed.

In Jose's house, as in most houses along the river, we find many tin cans. No one throws away a can in the Amazon Valley; it can be used for too many things. There are cans in the kitchen, five-gallon kerosene tins and smaller ones as well, full of water drawn from the river. This water is used for everything—drinking, washing, and cooking. The drinking water is often kept in earthen jugs to keep it cool; but in many homes there is only one dipper, which is used by everyone.

One of our jobs on the *Luzeiro* was to try to change these drinking habits. Today, there are many homes where, alongside the tin of water, is a board with a different cup for each member of the family and no one drinks from the dipper itself.

Jose's stove is a simply made structure of brick covered over with a long cast-iron plate in which holes have been made for the pots. Such a stove may be ten or even twelve feet long, and the wood burned in it is usually cut into ten-foot lengths. A hole at one end of the stove serves as a flue but it is almost never used, and the kitchen is frequently as steamy and smoky as an old-fashioned coal-burning engine room.

On top of every stove is the beanpot, which in some kitchens is never washed. Each morning more beans are added to what may have been left from the previous day. One of our major tasks—it was particularly Jessie's job—was to teach the river folk to keep their pots and pans shining clean. Jose and Maria always did; but along the river this was not always so. We also brought in many hundreds of toothbrushes for the river people.

One curious, but practical, Amazon custom is that of using orange peels to start fires. The peel of the Brazilian orange contains an acid that burns readily. Paper is at a premium, but oranges are available everywhere. To start a fire in the morning, all Maria has to do is to throw a few orange peels into the stove and strike a match.

Most of these homes have very few dishes, and these are reserved for special occasions. For everyday use, there are gourds. To make sure he doesn't run short, Jose, like every other home-owner, plants a few gourd trees around his house. They grow up to be about the size of orange trees and bear fruit which is sometimes as big as a watermelon.

When the gourd is ripe it is pulled off the tree and cut in half. After the inside has been scraped out, the two halves are left to dry in the sun. According to their size, they can be used for any kind of dish or cup. They can be painted with charming designs or initials. On many tables there will be large gourds full of manioc flour, or rice, or beans.

In the kitchen the gourds are usually kept in long, neat rows on a special shelf, upside down, so that if anything falls from the palm-leaf roof, any small snake or insect particularly, it won't land in somebody's dinner plate.

Gourds are useful not only as dishes but also as monkey traps. When a hole is cut in a round gourd and a banana put inside, the monkey will reach in for it and, once he has hold of the fruit, won't let go. With his paws in the gourd, he can't climb, but he hasn't the sense to let go the banana inside the gourd. He screams and screeches—but he can easily be caught.

In most of Brazil, especially in the wonderful cities of the south, the people are highly cultured, and living conditions rival anything in America. But along the Amazon it is a different story. For example, an Amazon house does not usually have a dining room or silverware. Meals are, in fact, one vast informality along the river.

Each person takes what he likes from the table—farina and beans and rice—and puts it in his gourd, and he mixes all this up into little balls. Then, with the farina spoon, which is probably the only implement on the table, he flips this Amazon farina-burger into his mouth so cleverly that the spoon never touches his lips and can therefore be used by the next in line.

Of course, like everyone else in Brazil, Jose and Maria drink coffee, but theirs is a real home brew. They buy the coffee bean green, put the two halves of the berries into an iron kettle, and cook and stir them until they are black— not brown, as in the States, but black as the Rio Negro. Then they add brown sugar and stir until each bean is glazed. They use a mortar to grind it fine, then boil it, and serve the dark, thick final product in cups about one fifth the size of ours.

They drink it black.

Breakfast, which they call *café*, is usually just a cup of this powerful brew with, possibly, a piece of bread on the side. For a tasty dessert, they fill a demitasse—gourd, of course—with sugar and pour coffee over it.

None of the river people have much modern equipment. Refrigerators, washing machines, these are almost unknown. Often the kitchen will have only a dirt floor, and often the rest of the house, too. Often they make their own soap out of the pods of the cacao bean. It is cheap, dark, and not very good for the hands.

Each family or individual has his private piece of water front. There he keeps his canoe; there he gets his water; there he—or she—washes the clothes. This they call their "port."

Laundry, for Maria, is no simple matter of filling a

machine, turning a switch, and having the clothes come out bright and shining. She lugs her wash down to the river, wets it, rubs on some of her homemade black soap, dips the clothes back into the water, and then pounds them on a board. More water . . . more soap . . . more pounding. This goes on until, as one woman explained to Jessie, "When there's no more buttons on them, then you know they're clean."

Maria has never heard of a dryer, and doesn't have a clothesline. Her wash is hung on the wooden fence that Jose has built to keep the cattle away from the house. And when ironing time comes, she stokes up her charcoal iron, lights it, and goes to work. These implements, usually five or six inches high, are heated from the inside and it's quite a chore just to get one lighted. Some ladies use a palm leaf as a bellows. The ashes are apt to fall out, too, but many times I have had a white linen suit washed and pressed by this method and have been surprised at how white and immaculate it turned out.

Always there are fruits around the house—especially bananas. Often you would see bunches of bananas in various stages of ripening in several corners of the kitchen or the main room. You never wait until they are ripe to pick them; by that time the birds will have spoiled them.

Mealtime along the Amazon is as informal as the meals themselves, and few people bother to sit down. People drift in and out. One will finish eating as another begins, and meanwhile the mother will be calling the rest of her brood from the fields or the riverbanks. I recall one woman who gave us a wonderful dinner; she had a birthday cake and other delicious foods to go with it, and she had gotten out her best tablecloth and dishes from the trunk for this occasion. We did not have chairs, but sat on benches along the table. As soon as she put the food on, however, one of the men of the house had to get a switch and stand behind us with it to keep the cats off the table while we ate. I was pretty sure that they did not generally eat sitting around this table.

Most river families have little furniture and what they do have is in their living rooms. Sometimes they have a supply of logs and planks, to raise their floors as the river comes up. The floods would wreck good furniture, so they have very little. Generally a bench or so—or a few kerosene boxes (the ones in which the ten-gallon kerosene cans are shipped to Brazil—they look like soap boxes but are bigger).

Usually, too, somewhere in the house, possibly in the front room, is a sewing machine. All the women know how to sew. Often there is a little table, and if it is a Christian home it will have a Bible on it. A table is not to eat on, but to display the most precious belongings.

Most of the houses have no electricity. For illumination at night the people use little kerosene lamps made out of bottles. These bottle lamps, made by local tinners, have wicks that go down into the bottles, and sometimes even handles and little reflectors with holes in the middle, so they can be hung up on the wall with a nail.

All over the house are the hammock hooks, and everyone who goes out of an afternoon takes his sleeping paraphernalia with him. The hammocks have nets to keep out mosquitoes, but there is no linen problem. They don't use any. If it's hot the men take off their shirts. Otherwise, they sleep with their clothes on.

There are no windowpanes, of course. Plaited palm

leaves cover windows and door openings at night and are pulled up in the morning. When it storms, particularly in houses with palm-woven walls, the rain sweeps in.

The hard-working women of the Amazon world do the cooking and sweeping and sewing. Often I have seen them sweeping up their dirt floors with brooms made of corn husks. They sew well and most of them know how to make lovely pieces of lace. Despite their poverty, both men and women love beautiful things and have a wealth of their own in the world around them—the brightly plumaged birds, the exotic flowers, and the lush beauty of the jungle. In every house we found flowers—giant orchids, in tin cans on the wall; Brazilian varieties of wild bougainvillaea, deep purple and mauve; vine flowers of a hundred shades; tree blossoms of rare fragrance. These are a people whose love of nature in its most beautiful dress is a lifelong thing.

Most of the land on which the people live is owned by the government, because to have a deed they must have their holdings surveyed. But their rights are usually recognized if they have cleared off a space and built a home—with or without deed. When Henry Ford in 1929 attempted to set up a rubber-producing empire on a tremendous tract of land given him by the government along the Tapajoz River, he had to buy off hundreds of these "squatters" to get it going. (Although Ford did his best, it was simply too big a project for the river at that time, and was ultimately abandoned.)

There are virtually no cars along the river, except in Belém and Manaus, and no use for them, for roads are nonexistent. About two hundred and fifty miles of the Pan-American Highway, which goes through the state of Para, had been built by 1958. But beyond this, and the few roads

—mostly gravel or dirt—around the major cities, the super-highways of the Amazon remain a remote dream.

One piece of furniture found in every house along the river—and indeed in every Brazilian home—is a trunk, usually very handsome, with rounded top and high sides. Along the Amazon this is usually kept in the room where the owners sleep. Closets are rare; good clothes are folded away in the trunk, along with the fine laces, the best china, any silverware or other valuables. Often the trunk is made out of tin as a further guard against insects and the torrential rains.

The trunk is the safe-deposit vault, the strong box, the repository of all treasures. It also serves—with a clean towel on top—as a kind of sofa on which visitors may sit. Often one house will boast several trunks. When we held a meeting in such a home, all the benches and trunks were hauled into the main room to serve as seats.

The patterns are different from other places and other peoples, and they are the same, as good and evil are forever individual, and forever the same.

One night, coming upriver, we saw several canoes full of people heading for a party. There are often dances in the towns and in larger homes; sometimes a good deal of Amazon whisky is drunk and sometimes—just as on a Saturday night back in America—violence erupts.

On one canoe were painted the words "Amazon Jazz Band." We knew about the *reque-reque* music played with bamboo poles and sticks which is often held up as a substitute for what we call music. This is usually what is heard along the river—a combination of jungle rhythm, rhumba rhythm, and second-class American dance tunes, all in one.

At Jessie's urging I moved upriver a half hour to be out of hearing, and for a while we had a quiet night. About two o'clock we were awakened when a canoe bumped into our boat. "Senhor Leo, your friend Alexander is calling for you. He is dying and wants you to come at once."

"Where is he?" I asked. "What happened?"

"He's back in that house where they're having the dance. He had a fight and was stabbed three times with a knife and is bleeding to death."

We pulled anchor and with the messenger acting as pilot went down to a small house where we saw a light. There was Alexander, a man of about thirty years, lying in a hammock on the porch. He had been stabbed in the shoulder, the forearm, and the palm of the hand. Each stab wound had pierced all the way through. We heated water, cleaned the wounds, gave him a shot to coagulate the blood, and then filled the wounds with sterile sulfa powder, followed by a big shot of penicillin. Alexander murmured his thanks and an explanation. "We quarreled over a girl at the dance," he said. "He attacked me and I was forced to defend myself and kill him. He was drunk and I was sober."

There was a long pause. Then he said, "It is at a time like this that one remembers God."

I knew he meant it sincerely, but I reminded him that it would be a good idea to think of God before getting into a scrape that led him into taking the life of another creature.

He promised faithfully that from now on he would be different and that we could hold meetings in his house.

On our next stop there, three weeks later, we inquired about Alexander. He was fully recovered, we were told, and the man he thought he had killed was not dead at all but had fled into the woods thinking that he had killed Alexander.

I was pleased at the happy ending of this Amazon version of a roadhouse brawl.

CHAPTER 15

PERSONAL STORY

TO people reading our story, it must seem that Jessie and I were so involved in the lives of the river people that we had no lives of our own. Sometimes we would almost have agreed. And yet we know that it is not so. Under Jessie's crisp white uniform was a woman—calm and strong in time of emergency, but with all the usual feminine frailties. And I—though I was able to cope, I thought, with almost anything that arose—was certainly no different from other men.

We had treated thousands of cases of malaria, but when it struck us, we reacted exactly like anyone else: we lay in our beds, alternately shivering and burning with fever, and wondering if each moment was to be our last.

For seventeen years we had lived on the river and managed to avoid "the fever." But one night we were tired after a long hard day and when we returned to the *Luzeiro,* anchored in the harbor in Maués, I dropped down on the sofa without bothering to close the window screens. Several hours later I awoke and put them up but the damage had been done. Within nine days, both Jessie and I were running fevers of 105 degrees and were too sick even to treat ourselves.

We sent our boat boy into the city to get us a doctor.

When he arrived he shook his head. "After treating all those people for a little case of malaria," he said, "you get it yourselves and have to call in somebody else."

We both felt so terrible it was hard to speak. I heard Jessie say, "Doctor, it's not the same when you get it yourself."

I steeled myself and finally got out a question. "Doctor, do you think we ought to go to a hospital?"

He stood in the middle of the cabin. "There isn't a hospital in town that has the comfort you two have here. You're just acting like a couple of typical patients who want a little extra pampering."

Sick as we were—or thought we were—we managed a laugh at that because it was so completely true. "Now what do you have for malaria?" he asked, and when we gave him a list of the special drugs, he said, "Give yourself a dose of your own medicine and go to sleep."

We did just that and in the morning we were delighted, and maybe a little surprised, to find our medicines had worked just as well on us as on others. Before the day was over, we felt so much better that we were up and around.

The malaria had hit us shortly after the end of World War II, a conflict that had made as many changes in our lives as in those of any other parents. While uniforms blossomed like Amazon orchids on the streets of Belém, while American officials and technicians began zooming up and down the river in their launches, up in the gales of the North Atlantic, thousands of miles away, our son Jack was doing his part. And no parents watched the mails more closely than we.

Jack had been a junior at Pacific Union College when war broke out. He was inducted into the Navy and we were as proud as any father and mother in the southern hemisphere when he wrote us that he'd been present at the historic mid-Atlantic conference between President Roosevelt and Prime Minister Churchill.

And then we got word that he was being sent to Brazil. Like every other mother, Jessie hustled out to the kitchen and began cooking and baking as if her life depended on it, for he was already en route, and was landing in Belém by noon the next day.

So he flew to the land that had been his second home for so long. He had just one day to stop over in Belém with us—not nearly long enough to eat all the good food Jessie had got ready for him. Then he would be on his way, he told us, to Baía, where he was to be assigned to a post in the Naval Observer Corps.

He kept his most important news until the last. Before leaving the States, he said, he had fallen in love; he and his young lady planned to be married. Jessie cried a little, as women do, and I shook Jack's hand, as my Nebraska father had done years before, when I'd told him about Jessie.

We had to keep track of the romance through Jack's letters, and when he wrote us that he had been able to arrange for his bride-to-be to fly to Brazil to marry him, we were happy and sad all at once. Happy because of our son's happiness; sad because travel restrictions wouldn't allow us to be present at the ceremony.

But we were able to get our first look at our son's bride-to-be. She had a two-day stopover in Belém, and we were delighted to be with her during that time. However, one of the documents which I will always treasure is a telegram we received at that time from Jack in Baía: "DAD DON'T

TAKE AUDREY ON A TRIP ON THAT LUZEIRO BUT SEND HER AT
ONCE HERE TO BAIA YOUR SON JACK."

We did as ordered. Theirs was the first naval wedding in
Baía and it was a big celebration. They were married, as
Brazilian law requires, in a civil ceremony. Then the religious ceremony was performed by a Protestant minister,
and the young couple marched out of the church under
an international arch formed by the crossed swords of the
American officers on one side, the Brazilians on the other.

Meanwhile, our daughter Marian was still in the States,
and though we heard from her regularly, and treasured our
snapshots of her, I found it hard to believe that the lovely
young woman they portrayed was our little girl, the little
girl I had kissed good-by on a station platform in 1936,
while she cried inconsolably.

Marian had finished high school and was taking pre-nurs-
ing courses at the Washington Missionary College, near
Washington, D.C., when we received a letter one day that
gave us a real shock. Dr. Raymond Ernshaw, who had
written it, described himself as an intern at a hospital near
Washington, and his purpose in writing us was to ask,
formally, for our daughter's hand in marriage.

This news wasn't as startling to Jessie as it was to me,
for she had visited Marian in the States in 1939, just before
the war broke out. Besides, women have a sixth sense about
such things. But for me, how could I think of my little girl
as old enough to marry? And just who was this stranger
who wrote us like this? As we went up and down the river,
answering the white-towel calls for aid, I'm afraid my
mind was often on my daughter, and her plans for the
future.

Then came a letter from Marian filling in all the details

that the doctor had left out, and saying that she wanted us to come to the States so that her dad could perform the wedding ceremony.

The war was still going on and travel was almost impossible, but our son got me back to the States somehow on a naval transport and we managed to get Jessie on a seaplane that one of the rubber-development organizations was using to haul crude rubber up to the States. Marian was waiting for us in Miami when we arrived—on separate planes, one day apart—and we went together up to Washington, D.C., where Jessie and I met our prospective son-in-law, and gave him our stamp of approval. I married them in the Takoma Park Adventist Church; and Jessie and I headed back for the jungle, feeling a little sad and a good deal older. When Raymond was called by the Navy and sent to Guam, Marian stayed in Washington and finished her nursing course, but after the war we were able to get together for a joyous reunion. Marian and her husband made us extremely happy when they came to Rio de Janeiro, where for a time he served as a missionary doctor. They have since returned to the States and are now living and working together in Texas.

Seeing so much sickness about us, Jessie and I used to congratulate ourselves on our own good health. We took what precautions we could, of course, but we couldn't stop our work on account of rain or heat, or the dangers everywhere present along the Amazon. It was the years, eventually, which began to take a toll.

During our visit to the States in 1936, Jessie had to undergo an operation for the removal of her gall bladder, and the following year I, the rugged Nebraskan who had never even owned a pair of glasses, developed a terrible eye infection. I got to a specialist as soon as I could, and he gave me medicine which cleared up the condition. But when I returned to the States after the war, and had my eyes checked, I was stunned to hear the word "cataract," and the news that I would have to have them removed from both eyes. The medical profession isn't sure what causes this disease, but in my case they figured the cataracts might have developed from the bright glare of the Amazon waters over so many years of tropical sun.

We weathered both these interruptions to our life and continued with our work, only to hear, in 1957, the most dreadful word of all. . . .

We were living in the outskirts of Rio, and Jessie had remained at home while I went out alone. I was up the river from Belém, ready to leave on a long trip into Indian country when, just fifteen minutes before my scheduled departure, I received a telegram saying that Jessie was ill. If there had been any speed limits on the Amazon, I would have broken every one of them as I raced back to Belém. There the news was even worse: Jessie had cancer of the liver, I was told, and could not possibly survive.

I hurried back to Rio. I had made that trip dozens of times before, but it had never seemed so long. At home, our doctor told me it wasn't Jessie's liver but one kidney that was completely destroyed. Almost all such cases were cancerous, he added.

But I found that I was not alone in my grief and alarm. Our church set aside one Sabbath for fasting and prayers for Jessie's life. The operation was performed; Jessie survived it; and four days later word came back that there was not a sign of cancer in the kidney that had been removed.

Together, it seemed, we were to be allowed to complete

our years of work in the fastnesses of Brazil. Together, we were to be allowed to return to our native land.

In our part of the United States, young people leave the parental nest as soon as they are able to use their wings. Some settle in towns nearby; others fly farther—to other parts of the country. They marry and set up new homes. But summers, after the harvest, or at Christmas time, they visit back and forth and there are happy family reunions as the various members exchange news.

Far away on the Amazon, this was one of the things Jessie and I missed most. We came from large families, both of us, and letters went back and forth frequently, but it was not the same. To see our parents again, and our brothers and sisters with their families, became one of our longings.

In 1936, this wish had come true. We had ordered a new Ford, by mail, and it was waiting for us when we arrived in the States on that year's furlough. In it we drove out to Nebraska, where we spent happy days visiting with Jessie's relatives and mine, who still lived in the neighborhood of Odessa. My parents were more than seventy-five, and had never traveled much, and had not even seen some of their grandchildren, scattered throughout the West.

"How would you like me to drive you out to see them?" I asked my father one day.

"Fine," he said. "We'll go from place to place. It'll be a family reunion on the installment plan."

Through Nebraska and on to Wyoming we went, Jessie and the children, my parents and myself. A stop in Cheyenne to visit my oldest sister, Flo. Then on to Nevada and California and throughout the great West, where my seven brothers and sisters and their families lived.

In San Francisco, Dad got his first view of the ocean. As he stood looking at the vast expanse of the Pacific, he turned to me: "I have always wanted to see the ocean, son. That's one reason I came on this trip. To see my children again—and this ocean."

Back in Odessa, the train that would start me on the way to Washington, D.C., from where I would go on to New York and then to Brazil, was leaving at 3 A.M. We sat up that night around the fire and talked until almost midnight.

At two, when the alarm went off, Mother was already getting breakfast—fried eggs and potatoes, toast and hot chocolate. Father had his lantern all shined up and his old handcart ready to haul my bags, the one block to the station.

At the station we waited silently for a few minutes. Then we saw the headlight of the express coming down over the hill, and in the dark Father stood by the side of the rails waving his lantern until the train blew a blast on the whistle and ground to a halt. I said my good-byes and got on the train. From my window I could see them—Dad with his lantern, Mother with a shawl over her shoulders, holding onto Dad's arm.

It was the last time I ever saw them.

CHAPTER 16

FLEET ADMIRAL

IN 1956, when we left Belém and moved south to Rio, where I assumed active command of the fleet of boats we now had in operation in many parts of South America—most of them built on the design of the *Luzeiro* —we had lived in the river world twenty-seven years. This was our home: Belém and its people, the river and its people, its bends and its rains, its smells and sights, its villages and houses, its thousand byways interlaced like the vines along the banks.

In a way that one can never explain, we had put down our roots here; we were Americans in deed and in fact, yet we were Brazilians as well—we spoke the language and understood the ways, and were a part of those ways. Leaving meant breaking with much of our life, with friends of years. Before we went south to Rio, the American consul, Mr. George Coleman, gave us a reception in Belém. It seemed as if everyone in town who spoke English was there, neighbors and friends, the prominent and the obscure of the city, who knew our work and had been part of it.

They had made up a special book for us as a going-away present—a handsome volume of the works of famous American poets, with each poem in English on one side of the page, and in Portuguese on the other.

We left friends behind us in that city as close to us as any people on earth. And we left, too, a few changes in which our work had played a part. There were clinics along the river, and in Belém itself was a hospital we had built, operated by Brazilian doctors and nurses and fully recognized by the country's medical and governmental heads. Original funds for this institution were raised by gifts from our Sabbath schools all over the world—children who poured in a total of $51,000 in a single offering for this work. Additional funds were later provided. We bought a beautiful tract of land and I helped in the actual designing and building of this attractive two-story hospital with some forty-five beds, its own electric plant, nurses' home, two homes for doctors and their families. When it was dedicated in 1951, not a penny was owed on it.

People on the river who needed help thus had a place to which we could bring them—or send them—for more protracted treatment than the *Luzeiro* could provide. The hospital was open to people of all faiths, and our doctors often operated for free. In our hospitals, each mission contributes a certain amount to a fund available for those who cannot pay. Charges are made where people can afford to pay, but no one is ever denied medical care, whether he has money or not.

In Mato Grosso, I visited one of our special hospitals—one supported in part by Brazilian government funds—primarily for the treatment of a terrible fever prevalent in this state at altitudes of from one thousand to three thousand feet. This infection, known as savage fire or wildfire, produces a red rash which spreads over the whole body, with itching and pain that can drive the patient insane. For a long time this disease was considered incurable; at our hospital by the end of 1958 we were achieving close to 40 per cent cures, and were able to arrest the fever's progress in many other cases.

Although I personally had nothing to do with the construction of this hospital, I did feel a certain proprietory interest because the doctor in charge was the onetime mayor of the Amazon city where I was arrested for having failed to check out with postal officials at the previous port of call. Following studies, at our college in São Paulo, he had volunteered to direct the work in the midst of this fever-infested area of Mato Grosso.

Throughout all Brazil, our church has built hospitals. In São Paulo, we have one that concentrates on polio—Casa de Saúde Liberdade. We have another in the mountains on the outskirts of Rio. In Peru, we have hospitals in Lima and in Juliaca, where Dr. Howard Smith, formerly of California, has done wonderful work. And there are many others, and many smaller clinics, which are operated with Brazilian doctors and nurses and all the latest equipment.

The life of a missionary isn't all grim; there are moments of true joy and laughter. I recall a wedding in one of our major cities—one of our doctors and nurses were married in a ceremony we all attended. They were to stay that night at the hotel and start on their honeymoon in the morning.

However, we had planned a little joke. When the newly-weds arrived at the hotel, the clerk said he had no room for them. They insisted they had made reservations weeks in advance, but the clerk was "so sorry." There was some mistake, he said, some slip-up. The manager was called; he was a good friend of both bride and bridegroom, and extremely apologetic. "There isn't a room left," he insisted, "but don't worry—we'll take care of you, even if we have to put up cots in the front hall."

The poor bride was almost in tears when she looked around and saw all her friends there, including the business manager of the hospital. Then the young couple realized it was all a joke. The bridal suite was all ready for them, decorated with the loveliest flowers of the Amazon.

Once we had moved down to Rio, I made a number of trips to other parts of South America, exploring rivers and helping the workers and missionaries in these areas in whatever way I could, particularly with problems of boats, supplies, and relationships with local authorities.

As "admiral of the fleet," I had considerable administrative work. In 1956, I flew from Belém to Manaus and on to Pôrto Velho, deep in the interior, not far from the Bolivian border. We were trying to get medical work started in this district. I later flew to Iquitos, a Peruvian town 2,300 miles up the Amazon. It is the end of the line for large ships.

My new work of caring for all the boats gave me a chance to see the scope of our activity on the rivers and to try to standardize our equipment and our procedures so far as practicable. It gave me a chance also to see much of South America that I had not been able to visit earlier. In Peru, on a mountain slope, pours a spring that is said to be the very start of the Amazon, and I stood astride the tiny brooklet that grows into the mightiest river known.

Part of my travels took me into Paraguay. In its capital, Asunción, there are no water mains and no sewage system. I was invited to dinner there by one of our missionary couples, just arrived from the States. Their belongings had not yet caught up with them, and the wife cooked dinner on her only utensil—a waffle iron. In the front yard were two stone benches, between which she put two suitcases one on top of the other. That was our dinner table. She had a few cracked dishes someone had lent her, and she cooked up a meal of potatoes and vegetables and bananas—all on her waffle iron.

All the men in our party agreed that our lady missionary was a wizard at the waffle iron, and the whole incident symbolized a little the kind of life a missionary must be able and ready to accept.

Two of our missionaries who worked in the wildest area of the interior were Peruvians—Julio Gomez and his wife. They had gotten a foothold among some of the Purus Indians, and they had built a church and a school; the Indians had put up a few buildings; and together they had formed a real community. Gomez was the preacher and his wife taught school. With this village as his base, Julio worked his way into the wilder areas. One day, at one of his points of call, the Indians asked him to dinner. He was slightly nervous about going, as he did not know his hosts —or how truly friendly they might be—but he felt he should accept. After the meal he felt ill. Some of the Indians from his own area reached him and took him on the Binini River back to his home as quickly as they could.

They got Julio back just in time for him to die—of poison—in his wife's arms. In spite of this, his widow stayed on in that wild and hostile place where, one of our workers told me, the mosquitoes are so thick at night that they make a black covering on the outside of the mosquito nettings, and another said he woke up in the morning to see a seven-foot boa coiled around the pole that held up the house.

But Mrs. Gomez stayed and went on with the work in the school and church. Finally, the president of that district, Richard A. Heyden, went out by boat to that lonely place, where there was no one but she and the Indians, and suggested that she come down to the city of Iquitos, in Peru, where she could teach in one of our larger schools.

Certainly, he said, she would be happier living with people of her own culture and background. But Sister Gomez shook her head. "When we came here," she told him, with tears in her eyes, "we came because the Lord called us to work here with these Indians. The work is not done. He has called my husband but He has not called me yet, so I will stay here with our Indians."

When I heard this story and saw this woman, I asked myself: What have I done? What sacrifices have I made, in comparison to hers?

Yet some things were achieved in Brazil, and especially along the river, in which we played a part.

There is a new outlook in many parts of the river today, a new way of living and looking upon the world, a brighter, happier way. There is new health and new sanitation and better diet and hygiene. Standards have been lifted socially and physically and spiritually. Doctors are going there now, some on our boats, some entirely on their own. The Brazilian people and the government and churches are working together to make this brave new Amazon world a lasting reality.

The federal government of Brazil, in recognition of our role in this change, decorated both Jessie and me with the Brazilian Cross; the first time that a woman has been thus honored. This gleaming medal is one of the highest honors the government can bestow; to civilians it has the same aura as the American Congressional Medal of Honor. Our joy in receiving it came not from any personal or prideful preening but from the awareness, through this award, that our efforts and the work we had been allowed to do were understood and accepted in this land and among these people we had come to love as deeply as our own. The wording of the award they gave Jessie and me reached us in a telegram at a gathering of friends back in America, some months after our return from Brazil. The citation read: "For having awakened the Brazilian Government to the fact that, among the Amazon's rich resources, its peoples are the most important and that their health or ill health may well dictate whether Amazonia's potential is developed or left dormant."

But this was not all. In another unprecedented move, the Brazilian government voted the sum of almost a million dollars—$90,000 a year for ten years—to be given to our missions to continue and expand the boat work along Brazil's rivers. The North Brazil Union, the East Brazil Union, and the South Brazil Union of our church each get $30,000 a year—to be used solely for our work on those little white boats which ply the far reaches of the rivers.

This was a signal honor. Brazil is a land predominantly Catholic, yet it has the vision and tolerance and appreciation not only to accept but also to assist a Protestant missionary effort like our own—because of its meaning to the people.

That they have done this is a tribute to the substantial worth of our missions and the work of our launches along the river, carried on by Brazilian nationals and by American missionaries, teaming up to make the launch program a reality.

Governments do not normally extend such grants to foreign missions, religious or otherwise. This was a special recognition that the work of our church and of our launches extends beyond the boundaries of nation or formal creed or denomination.

There are no boundaries in the work of the Lord.

The launches stand at the heart of our work, the boats of burden that carried Jessie and me and our medicines— and later others like us and their supplies—along the dark rivers. Other *Luzeiros;* other bearers of light.

By the time we left there were five *Luzeiros* in South America, built exactly or basically on the pattern of the original, plying the Amazon, the mouth of the Amazon, the Maués and Paraná Ramos rivers, the Parnaíba. We have boats on the San Francisco River and the Araguaia, and several smaller boats for messenger work and the colporteurs.

All of these boats are manned by our own church members; all are now medically trained doctors or nurses. On the San Francisco, as we left Brazil, we had Charles Scofield and his wife—both Americans and both trained nurses. Scofield was treating 15,000 persons a year on that river alone. We had other boats in Peru and Bolivia, on the rivers of these countries.

In Asunción, Paraguay, in 1957, I gave a talk to an audience of almost a thousand about our work. This was not a religious meeting but a discussion of our medical mission on the boats. I also showed pictures of the launch work. When the meeting was over, a stocky, well-dressed man, in an immaculate white suit, came up to me and said, "I would like to talk to you for about an hour."

I had a very heavy program of meetings, and arranging an hour's time might be difficult. Yet I did not want to refuse anyone, so I asked, "Can we discuss whatever it is right here?"

"Well, if there is no other opportunity—right here," he said brusquely. He at once began talking over the possibility of a boat for the Paraguay River, which reaches up into Brazil. In the midst of our discussion, someone came up and greeted him, "Oh, how are you, General Yergers?"

I was talking to the most important and powerful military leader in Paraguay. His eyes sparkled as we discussed the boat. Finally he told me, "Listen, the day you Adventists put a boat on that river you come to me and we will give you all the help that the Paraguay government can give. All our machine shops, all our facilities will be at your command."

Shortly after I returned to America I received a letter from a doctor in California. He stated that he had been impressed to write me to state that he had $1,000 to give us toward building a new boat for work in a new place. With additional funds added, it seems likely as this is written that we will soon have a boat serving the people along the Paraguay River from Asunción, Paraguay, as far north as the obscure villages in the southwest corner of Mato Grosso, Brazil.

The Lord protects these boats—protects them and guides them.

Once we were delivering a newly built medical launch from Belém to the Parnaíba River, which flows east across the state of Piauí and empties into the Atlantic about 750 miles south of the mouth of the Amazon. To get there we had to take that thirty-six-foot flat-bottomed craft onto the Atlantic. There were several of us on board—including a licensed pilot we had hired for this dangerous journey.

En route we ran into one of the most terrible storms I have ever experienced. Sometimes we would be on top of the crest of a wave and the next instant we would plunge down into a trough and the waves would threaten to engulf us. The pilot was lashed to his post on top to keep from being swept into the sea by the waves that broke over our tiny decks.

We did not think we could stay afloat. We prayed for God's help. Off in the distance, on the shore, we made out what seemed like a river entrance. The river would give us refuge if we could reach it. We turned toward land. Soon we could see the white breakers, dashing against the rocks on both sides of the narrow entrance of the river, and hurling spume and spray high into the air.

Sometimes we would ride on top of the crest and then we would spin downward, halfway turned around; it was almost impossible to hold on course. Finally, one giant breaker lifted us like a toy boat, swirling us forward into the river. And suddenly it was calm. We were in one of the most restful havens I had ever seen. For the first time in five days, we were able to have a peaceful night's sleep.

When we awoke in the morning, our boat was surrounded by scores of people in canoes. They all wanted to know who we were and what we wanted. When we told them, they said there was a Protestant church in their village and would we have a service there? Elder Fred Pritchard played a few solos on his saxophone, and we joined him then on our portable organ. And more canoes kept coming. One large canoe appeared with about thirty-five people on it and a man standing in the prow with a high stiff collar and a Bible under his arm. This was the Protestant group they had told us about.

Pastor Pritchard leaned over to me and whispered, "I'll have to preach them a sermon. I hadn't planned on this. What shall I tell them?"

I told him, "Preach the Message—and make it plain."

Fred did. He preached one of the finest sermons I ever heard and when it was over—before we left to complete in safety the rest of our journey—the tall pastor we had first seen put his arm around us and said, "Now I know why the Lord sent that storm and forced you into this river. It was to bring us this message from the Scripture."

The story of the white launches has spread even beyond South America. In other missionary areas, our church and missions of other churches are using the same basic design of the original *Luzeiro* for new boats to penetrate new areas, wherever there is need for people to come with help and medical supplies—and faith.

Letters come to Jessie and me from others starting out to these far-off places—letters asking for guidance and suggestions, and plans whereby they can build a *Luzeiro* in some other part of South America, or in Africa or Asia. We send them whatever plans we have, and information and

suggestions, all the information we have available. There
is no copyright on the *Luzeiro* pattern or design; it is
available to any who wish to use it in the service of others.

So today there are a number of *Luzeiros*, of various
modified designs and plans, treading the dark rivers of
the world in Burmese jungles and off the coast of China,
manned by Adventists and missionaries of other denomina-
tions as well—wherever young adventurers of faith may go.

Other *Luzeiros* in other lands. Varied in size and con-
tour, yet basically the *Luzeiro* pattern. A dozen or more,
perhaps, from the heavy correspondence that comes in to
us, queries and occasional reports about the launches,
from scattered areas of the globe.

The Light Bearers have reached beyond Jessie and me,
beyond Brazil, to the farthest corners of the world. . . .

When we were in Charles City, Iowa, one of my close
friends was a man named George Byrd, who worked with
me at the tractor company. When I was trying to decide
whether to go into missionary work, George opposed the
idea, and told me I was throwing away my life.

I was an electrician and a technological expert, he told
me, and I could make a fortune in that kind of work, but
what could I ever hope to make as a missionary? I remember how he called me into his office and tried to make me
change my mind. But the more he talked the more I was
certain that he was wrong. I remember telling him, "There
are different values—and different goals for each of us."

When Jessie and I left America for the Amazon, we lost
track of many people, including this man and his wife.
But in the mid 1950's they read a story about our work.

Not long afterward, I had a letter from him, then a long radiogram.

Our life sounded so fantastic, he wrote, that he wanted to know more about it. He and his wife were flying down to Brazil for a vacation. Could they come to see us? And where should they go and how? I radioed four words: "Will meet plane Rio."

We had a wonderful reunion with them, told them what we had been doing all through the years; and took them out for a journey on one of our boats, back into the green world we had known for so long.

One slightly embarrassing situation involved translation of a sermon for George on a Sabbath morning in Rio, when George and his wife, as well as a young American doctor and his wife, attended services with us at our Central Church.

Neither visiting couple understood Portuguese—in which, of course, the minister preached the sermon. One of our officials, Pastor Wilcox, translated for the doctor and his wife, while I translated for George and his wife. I didn't think the sermon that morning was particularly exciting, so I paid no attention to what was being preached and—pretending to translate—I preached a sermon of my own.

In the course of this "translation," to illustrate a point about how often we cheat ourselves, I told of a man hired to build a house, who tried to cheat his employer by buying the cheapest materials and charging for the best, only to learn that his employer, in gratitude for the man's faithfulness, was giving him the house.

George was impressed by my story and later that day, when we were all at dinner, he mentioned the illustration as one of the best things in the sermon. The doctor looked startled and said to Pastor Wilcox, "I don't remember that story. You didn't translate anything like that, Pastor Wilcox."

Wilcox started to ruffle but then he looked at me and caught my high sign. "Well," he said, gently, "I guess we each have to translate according to our own interpretation."

But the glance he gave me indicated some doubt as to how far afield an interpreter's interpretation has a right to roam.

Later, on one of our boats on the San Francisco River, we showed George and his wife how our missionary doctors handle patients. In one afternoon the doctor on that boat took care of more than seventy-five patients, and also set up a dental clinic where patients were treated so expeditiously that George finally suggested, "Why don't we get our old doc from Charles City down here and let him take lessons? We just can't pull teeth that fast in Iowa."

What he saw of our work there in Brazil impressed him as deeply as any experience of his life, George confided during that trip.

He had risen in the world of industry to become the owner of a large factory. He was successful and wealthy and respected in his chosen field.

"I'm a big financial success and I have all the worldly things I need." he told me. "Remember when I tried to talk you out of all this? Remember when I told you that you were crazy—and were making the worst mistake of your life?"

I nodded. Looking out across the water, he went on, "Let me tell you, I was the one who was wrong. You took the only road that counts, and what you have done is worth far more than a dozen fortunes you might have made in industry."

My industrialist friend smiled. The green world around us was quiet and pleasant in the early evening.

CHAPTER 17

AMAZON EPILOGUE

THERE are moments that stand as symbols, even though they may not fall neatly into the proper chronological order. After we left the Amazon for Rio, there were many months of great activity before we returned to the States for good, in the spring of 1958. Yet for us the moment of moments came on the Amazon on the day we turned over command of the *Luzeiro* to Walter and Olga.

It did not matter that my work continued, that now I was in charge of all the boats, including this one. This had been our home, this boat; leaving it was like saying good-by to a friend of long years' standing, a sharer of adventures and terrors, defeats and triumphs and joys.

We tied up at the little dock as Walter and Olga stood facing me. I took off my hat and handed it to him. He put it on. Perhaps it would have seemed like a silly ceremony to anyone looking on; to me, to us, it was meaningful. A palm leaf rustled on the bank. The river waters lapped against the dock. As I looked at Olga, in my mind's eye I saw her as a baby—an infant on a bright satin cushion years ago, at our first Sabbath service in Rio.

I shook hands with Walter and kissed Olga on the cheek. They turned and boarded the boat, and Jessie and I stood there alone on the dock and watched the *Luzeiro* pull away, out into the stream. Walter and Olga waved at us, but as they rounded a bend, we were alone, and the sound of the *Luzeiro*'s motor grew fainter in the distance.

The world around us was not the same as that to which Jessie and I had come, as young missionaries, more than a third of a century before.

The differences were to be seen not on the surface only, for they were many and far-reaching; the whole life of the river and its people had changed. No longer was it a world of rampant disease and filth, neglect, despair, hopelessness, and death.

No longer was it a world of malaria epidemics, of a little boy in a canoe gliding through the moonlight to tell us of the epidemic that had taken most of his family and the people in his village. Malaria had not been wiped out, but it was under control.

So also were many of the other diseases. Hookworm and yaws particularly, while not defeated, were no longer the dreadful scourge that they had been.

It was a world of new meanings. In many places now, where there had been nothing, there were churches and schools. Youngsters who might have died of some tropical fever, or survived somehow in the midst of superstition and violence and murder, today are going to school, learning to read and write, and perhaps, as many now do, go on to higher education in the colleges and universities in the south.

There are new ideas along the river, about hygiene and cleanliness and the value of water in keeping an infection clean, the ways of living and cooking and eating. On a Sabbath morning in many of the river towns you will see scores of people, sometimes more than a hundred, on their way to church, whole families and communities, in their white Sabbath-come-to-meeting clothes.

There is a happiness about these people, and it is no false happiness, you will find, if you talk with them. There is an excitement and a joy that was not there when Jessie and I first arrived; it is the joy of people who have found inner understanding and peace. For many of these people have come to know Christ and His love.

This is the heart of the change that has come to them—this awakening. They did not care before. They had no reason to care, because so far as they knew no one bothered about them. They were here alone on the Amazon to rot away, and no one would care.

Now they knew better, for they had seen and learned that there were those who cared; and they have learned about the love of God, and the power and meaning it can have for each of them. This was the message that we brought to them, as others did also. We had come to bring His Word—and to bring this love in action.

We worked with the tools we were given; and we asked no glory and no profit except to serve. We tried to teach the adults and to instruct the young, to improve their lives and their chances for the future.

With full awareness of our own human frailties—too many even to begin to count—we sought nevertheless to put aside our personal wishes, to do what we could, to stop wherever and whenever the white towel waved along the bank, to go under whatever circumstances we had to face when we were needed by the sick, the injured, the frightened, the lost.

In some measure, we had helped to lead these people of the riverways out of their own shadows. It was a work in which both Jessie and I could be glad and grateful to have played a part.

Along the river, in any village or city, in almost any home, they knew about Dona Jessie and Senhor Leo, the medical missionaries in the white boat. Some could tell you little stories of having had a dinner with us on the boat and tasted some of Dona Jessie's wonderful Brazilian cooking.

Or they could tell you about an alligator shoot with Senhor Leo, or hunting wild ducks, or deer and jaguars and tortoise, or fishing. Or some of the stories of the boat boys we had had or the storms we had weathered, or our moments of peril in distant corners of the great riverway.

All of this, too, the excitement and adventure, the traveling, the most remote areas, the wild Indian territory; the great cities of the south—all of this was a part of what we lived and experienced, and a hundred scattered meanings and incidents seemed to flood my thoughts in those moments of leaving the river, that day.

It had been a joyous and unique experience and opportunity. We had been privileged to work in many instances on an elemental level, with the basic, still unhardened clay of human beings, and to help them find their ways.

As we stood there on the river dock, there came into my mind familiar words, words that had long been a symbol, a standard of the road all of us should seek to follow, the way He pointed out to each of us in His words about the final judgment:

"Then shall the King say unto them on his right hand, Come, ye blessed of my Father, inherit the kingdom prepared for you from the foundation of the world:

"For I was an hungred, and ye gave me meat: I was thirsty, and ye gave me drink: I was a stranger and ye took me in:

"Naked, and ye clothed me: I was sick, and ye visited me: I was in prison, and ye came unto me.

"Then shall the righteous answer him saying, Lord, when saw we thee an hungred, and fed thee? or thirsty, and gave thee drink?

"When saw we thee a stranger, and took thee in? or naked, and clothed thee?

"And the King shall answer and say unto them, Verily, I say unto you, Inasmuch as ye have done it unto the least of these my brethren, ye have done it unto me."

The beauty and depth of these words clung in my thought. *Unto the least of these my brethren.* The hush of the jungle and its people seemed to close around us.

It was growing late. Jessie slipped her arm through mine. We would have to hurry to make our plane at the airport. The *Luzeiro* was out of sight in the harbor.

If we were sad at this leave-taking, we also found joy in the vast changes that had brought to the river world a new meaning and a new start—a new chance to grope its way to high heaven, out of its steaming Green Hell.

This fact was uppermost in our thoughts as Jessie slipped her arm through mine and we turned away.

In a little while, night would close in and, beyond the harbor, Walter and Olga would anchor near shore and the endless music of the Amazon night would begin again.